Wok Time!

© Naumann & Göbel Verlagsgesellschaft mbH, a subsidiary of
VEMAG Verlags- und Medien Aktiengesellschaft, Cologne
www.apollo-intermedia.de

Complete production: Naumann & Göbel Verlagsgesellschaft mbH, Cologne
Printed in Poland

ISBN 3-625-11095-4

Wok Time!

NAUMANN & GÖBEL

CONTENTS

COOKING WITH THE WOK

Asia's number one cooking utensil is no longer a stranger to European kitchens. This multi-talented pan, used in stir-frying, steaming, frying, stewing, and deep-frying, brings together the best of both European and Far Eastern tastes. Discover for yourself the unlimited possibilities the wok holds, and see how easily, quickly and healthily you can use it to prepare the most delightful recipes.

A Wok Goes around the World

The wok owes its creation to the poverty-stricken population of rural China about 3000 years ago. The lack of fuel for fires created a need for an effective and economical way to prepare daily food. A pot (in Cantonese, "wok") with a special manner of cooking, which allowed for speedy frying of food over strong heat, was invented. The iron cooking utensil, shaped like a half sphere, was able to use the heat from the fire pit at optimal efficiency, provided for lightning-speed and consistent preparation of chopped-up ingredients. This style of preparation, in which the ingredients are stirred around the curved sides of the wok in a small amount of very hot oil, is called "chow" – stirring in the pan. Besides imparting a rich flavour, this style of preparation is also quite healthy, as, due to the short amount of time the ingredients are actually over the flame, flavour, vitamins and nutrients are allowed to remain in the food.

Fast, healthy and delicious: small wonder that the wok soon spread over the borders of China to become Asia's number one cooking utensil. In typical Asian street kitchens as well as in restaurants or at home, the wok is no longer an instrument to be dismissed. In Europe, too, the wok is at long last unknown no more. Here, in the search for a modern, well-balanced diet, the sensible culinary culture of the Far East has won as the accepted role model. The freshness, ease of preparation, simplicity and balance of flavour and texture that are all still integral components of the Asian cooking tradition are as good as anything offered by the advances of modern dietary science, and they have found their way into the European kitchen in "Fusion Cooking." In this way, the wok has become not only a symbol of Far Eastern culture, but also a bond between the cooking traditions of Europe and Asia.

The sheer breadth of possibilities for using the wok make it a sort of universal utensil, able to be put to a specific use in each different kitchen. Besides stir-frying, it also lends itself to broiling and stewing, and is ideal for deep-frying and steaming any ingredients. All in all the wok is an all-around ally for the cook, and an integral part of the healthy modern kitchen.

The Modern Wok

As the wok has become more familiar to European cooks, both its materials and design have changed to better suit their needs. The traditional Chinese wok is made of iron, and its rounded bottom means that it can only be set upon certain types of stoves.

Today's wok is designed for the modern kitchen: a wok with a curved underside can only be used with gas stoves, and for such use a special "collar" provides the necessary positioning to the flame. In the meantime, the bottoms of woks meant for use on electric stoves are flat and smooth.

The **materials** used for different woks range from rust free stainless steel to aluminium and copper to carbon steel. Most woks are also treated with a coating that allows for easy cleaning. Be careful, however, not to damage the protective coating of the inner walls by using hard-edged stirring utensils. It is better to use spatulas and scrapers made of wood or bamboo.

When choosing a wok for your kitchen, it is important that the metal absorb heat rapidly and also react quickly to changes in temperature. Copper and aluminium are especially good for such reasons, although woks made of copper are admittedly often quite expensive.

Please note that any woks untreated with a protective coating must be prepared before use. When doing this, it's best to follow the directions that came with your wok to the letter, as only then can you be assured of getting the best out of your wok.

The proper **size** of the wok depends entirely on your individual cooking habits. It is worth noting that a large wok can be ideal for the preparation of very small meals, but the reverse does not hold. Experience states that to prepare four portions one needs a wok from about 35 to 40 cm across.

Accessories

Besides the wok itself, there are naturally a variety of accessories available to make cooking and preparing food with the wok simpler and easier. Most woks are sold as similar sets. Anything further that you need can be found in shops specialising in Asian imports or in any department or household wares store.

Metal Grille

Usually half-round in shape, a metal grille is among the essential accoutrements for any wok. It hangs from the upper rim of the wok, so that cooked food drips onto it, while at the same time staying warm.

Cover

A cover is also among the essential accessories for any wok. Usually made from stainless steel, aluminium or heat resistant glass, it is used primarily for steaming.

Spatula

The spatula looks like a small shovel with upraised lips. The lower edge of the metal blade is gently rounded, to facilitate stirring and the lifting up of food. The handle of the spatula is quite long, and made of wood or artificial material.

Straining Spoon and Bamboo Strainer

There are two types of strainers. A straining spoon, with a wire mesh ranging from fine to wide and a handle of bamboo or wood, is used to retrieve food from the cooking fat or to stir ingredients around in hot oil in order to achieve a consistent browning. Additionally there are bamboo strainers in various sizes, with or without drainers, as well as smaller mesh strainers with handles or bamboo grips.

Cooking Chopsticks

These chopsticks are used by true virtuosos to stir the food in the wok. They are longer than normal chopsticks, so you can reach the bottom of the wok without frying your fingers.

Bamboo Tongs

With the tongs, you can sneak small test bites while cooking or easily retrieve fully-cooked food from the wok. The tongs are especially useful for anyone who has not quite learned the fine points of using chopsticks.

Bamboo Brush

The traditional brush is also a helpful accessory, useful for many tasks. You can use the brush to stir very finely minced ingredients around the pan, as the fine ends of the brush lend themselves to this better than the large spatula. Additionally, one may clean the wok with the help of the brush under hot running water. The brush, made of bamboo fibre, should be cleaned well after use (although never with washing-up liquid), and left to air dry.

Steaming Basket

Steaming is the most widely-used method for preparing vegetables and fish in China. The bamboo steaming baskets used, available in various sizes, are fastened and placed into the wok above boiling water. The rising steam permeates the basket without allowing water to come into contact with the food. As the steaming baskets are not only useful but also attractive, they are often used when arranging the food for presentation.

Cleaver

An Asian cleaver, together with an appropriate chopping board, is necessary for anyone wanting to cook fearlessly and according to true Asian style. Such cleavers are widely used in Asian cooking. Besides fine and coarse chopping, the cleaver is also useful for filleting, pounding and tenderizing meat. Asian chefs keep three separate cleavers in the cupboard, differentiated according to size and type.

Chopping Board

A good cleaver naturally requires a good solid chopping board. In the Asian kitchen round slabs of hardwood are used, cut from a single block. The boards or blocks available in Europe, made of layers of wood held glued together or fastened with pegs, are ideal. A good chopping board does not come cheaply, but given proper care and cleaning will last as long as the cleaver itself.

Cooking with the Wok

Stir Frying

Stir frying is the most well known and popular way to prepare food in the wok. The ingredients are heated in a very small amount of very hot oil, and then stirred round constantly. It takes only a few minutes to prepare dishes this way and the ingredients do not lose their natural flavour or vitamins and nutrients. Meat is crispy on the outside but stays succulent on the inside. Vegetables stay crunchy and firm. Since stir frying is quite a speedy affair, it's important to have all ingredients already prepared and handy before you begin. Ingredients which require a longer cooking time should be the first to go in the wok, followed later by those needing less time. It's also sensible to chop the ingredients that require a shorter cooking time less finely than those that need more.

Braising

Braising is a process by which only smaller amounts of ingredients are cooked or intensely fried in the wok, and then afterwards doused in liquid (water, spiced stock, etc.) and left to simmer beneath a closed cover. This method of preparation is especially useful for coarse meats.
Red cooking, also a type of braising, is a typical Chinese style of cooking. The name comes from the use of dark liquids, such as soy sauce, in which the food is braised after being fried for a short time.

Deep Frying

In deep frying, ingredients – either raw or battered – are fried in hot oil. The wok is especially suited for this, as one need not use the great amount of oil for deep frying in the wok that is required for conventional methods. Deep frying in the wok is in fact child's play, if the oil is the correct temperature. To determine if this is the case, simply immerse a wooden chopstick into the oil; if blisters appear on the wood, you can start frying.

Steaming

The most classic style of preparing food in China is steaming it. With this method, ingredients are placed into the rinsed steam baskets, which are then placed in the wok with a small amount of water and allowed to absorb the steam. When steaming it is important that the food and steaming baskets not come into contact with the water in the wok and that the wok is well sealed. You should also make sure you repeatedly check the level of the water while the steaming is going on.

Boiling

The wok is not called multi-talented in vain. Naturally one may also use it to prepare soups and hotpots, in which the ingredients are first quickly fried and then covered with a liquid and allowed to boil.
In a complex but delightful process, one may prepare meat in the wok by means of first broiling, and then frying it. The inside of the meat stays tender, and the exterior gives rise to a crisp shell.

Smoking

Here, too, the wok proves useful. Line the wok with a layer of aluminium foil and place a small amount of smoking chips on top of it. When the wok is sufficiently preheated, place the food to be smoked on top of a grill or a screen insert above the foil. When used for smoking, the wok must be securely fastened, so that no smoke is allowed to escape.

You will learn which spices and herb to use in each unique dish's respective recipe. These exotic ingredients are to be found in shops specialising in Asian imports or well-stocked specialty stores. Our wok recipes primarily reflect Asian cooking with its emphasis on fresh vegetables, rice, noodles, fish and poultry, but also contain European ingredients and dishes that can be improved upon by Asian aroma and flavour. Discover the many uses of your wok and enjoy the unification of European and Asian tastes.

HEALTHY & VEGETARIAN

Freshness and simplicity are the essential ingredients of Asian cuisine. Because of this, vegetables, spices and fruit possess a special significance. These ingredients can be cooked to perfection in the wok in a matter of minutes, without losing their natural flavours, vitamins or minerals.

BAKED COURGETTE

■ Serves 4

1 3/4 lb courgette

5 1/4 oz ground cashews

1 3/4 oz grated Parmesan

1/2 bunch coriander

1 egg

salt

pepper

3 tbsp peanut oil

14 1/2 oz sour cream

3 1/2 oz yoghurt

1 garlic clove

1 small red pepper

powdered ginger

cumin powder

Preparation time: approx. 30 minutes
816 cal/3430 kJ

1 Wash and dry the courgette, then cut it lengthwise into thin slices. Mix the cashews with the cheese. Wash and dry the coriander, then chop finely and mix in with the cheese as well.

2 Whisk the egg in a bowl, adding salt and pepper. Dip the courgette slices thoroughly in the egg, afterwards turning them over in the cheese mixture. Press down lightly on the panade.

3 Heat up the oil in the wok and fry the courgette slices until golden brown.

Mix the sour cream and the yoghurt together in a separate bowl. Peel the garlic clove and press it into the mixture of sour cream and yoghurt.

4 Wash the red pepper, cut it in two and remove the seeds. Cut the remainder into very small cubes, and mix into the dip. Be sure to flavour the dip with salt, pepper, ginger and cumin. Arrange the courgette slices on plates with the dip, and serve.

Cashews

The soft seed of the cashew tree, with its unique, sweet, almond-like flavour, is used for many purposes in Asian cuisine. Since the nuts, with their stomach-settling and nerve-invigorating properties, are easily ground into powder, they are primarily used, as in this recipe, for panades instead of as meal.

SPICY BEAN SOUP

■ **Serves 4**

1 lb 5 1/4 oz green beans
1 bunch basil
2 tbsp peanut oil
3 1/2 oz bacon bits
5 1/4 oz diced tomatoes
3 tbsp soy sauce
2 tbsp Hoisin sauce
1 pint 7 fl oz vegetable stock
2 garlic cloves
salt, pepper
cumin powder

Preparation time:
approx. 20 minutes
255 cal/1072 kJ

Soy Sauce
The basic spices of many Asian dishes are based on soy sauce, a traditional flavouring sauce with the potential for universal use. The character of the sauce changes according to country of origin; for this reason, when preparing Japanese dishes, you should use Japanese sauce, and for Chinese dishes use Chinese soy sauce.

1 Wash the beans under cold running water, remove the stems and cut the beans in two. Wash the basil, allow it to dry and cut it into strips. Heat the peanut oil in the wok and place the bacon in it to fry.

2 Add the beans, basil and tomatoes to the oil. Season with soy sauce and Hoisin sauce. After about 4 minutes, add the vegetable stock.

3 Peel the garlic cloves and press them into the wok. Allow everything to cook for approximately five more minutes. Before serving, flavour with salt, pepper and cumin.

SWEET AND SOUR PEPPERS

■ **Serves 4**

2 each of red, yellow and green peppers
4 tomatoes
6 garlic cloves
1/2 bunch parsley
3 tbsp peanut oil
4 tbsp rice wine
4 tbsp soy sauce
1 tbsp sugar
aniseed, coriander and ginger powder

Preparation time:
approx. 20 minutes
255 cal/1072 kJ

Peanut Oil

Peanut oil can be heated to very high temperatures without ill effects, and is therefore ideal for frying and deep frying in the wok. Unlike sesame oil, it has a neutral flavour.

1 Wash and scrub the peppers, remove the pips and cut them into thin slices.

2 Cut the tomatoes crosswise, immerse quickly in boiling water, drain, peel and cut into wedges.

3 Peel and press the garlic cloves. Wash and dry the parsley, then chop it finely into flakes.

4 Heat the peanut oil in the wok and add the vegetables to stew. Pour in the rice wine and the soy sauce.

5 Allow to cook for a short time, and season with sugar, aniseed, coriander and ginger powder. Arrange on plates and serve.

LENTIL SALAD

■ **Serves 4**

2 onions
1 bunch scallions
3 1/2 oz roasted peanuts
1/2 bunch watercress
3 1/2 oz couscous
3 tbsp sesame oil
7 oz red lentils
salt
sugar
3 tbsp white wine vinegar
1 tbsp soy sauce
8 3/4 fl oz vegetable stock

Preparation time:
approx. 25 minutes
374 cal/1571 kJ

1 Peel the onions and cut into cubes. Wash the scallions and slice into rings.

2 Chop the peanuts coarsely. Clean the watercress, and pluck off the leaves.

3 Prepare the couscous according to the packaging instructions. Heat the peanut oil in the wok and add the onions, scallions and nuts to stew.

4 Add the lentils and flavour the wok with salt, sugar, white wine vinegar and soy sauce.

5 Pour in the vegetable stock and allow everything to cook for around 4 minutes over low heat.

6 Stir the couscous and the watercress together. Place the couscous and the ingredients from the wok together on plates and serve lukewarm with a small amount of watercress as garnish.

Watercress

Watercress grows in moist areas such as on the banks of streams or near rivers. The savoury, bitter flavour goes very well with salads and meat dishes. Watercress should always be cooked for only a short time with the entrée.

FRIED VEGETABLES

■ Serves 4

3 red onions
2 garlic cloves
2 small aubergines
2 small courgettes
4 flesh tomatoes
2 peppers
4 tbsp sesame oil
salt
ground pepper
mustard seeds
cumin powder
1–2 stalks Thai basil
1–2 stalks
lemon grass or
1 tbsp dried
lemon grass
17 1/2 fl oz
vegetable stock
2/3 tbsp hulled
sesame seeds

Preparation time:
approx. 25 minutes
480 cal/2017 kJ

1 Peel both the onions and the garlic cloves and cut into small cubes. Wash the aubergines and courgettes, slice them in half lengthwise and cut into centimetre-thick triangles.

2 Cut the tomatoes crosswise, immerse for a short while in boiling water, drain and remove the skin. Cut the tomatoes in two, remove the seeds and cut into small pieces. Cut the peppers in two, remove the pips and wash in cold running water. Cut into large pieces.

3 Heat the oil in the wok and fry the vegetables separately from each other for about 2–3 minutes. After all the vegetables have been fried, combine them together in the wok and season with salt, pepper, mustard seeds and cumin.

4 Wash the herbs and chop finely. Add the chopped herbs and the vegetable stock to the vegetables and allow to cook for 2–3 minutes.

5 Roast the sesame seeds in a pan. Put the vegetables onto plates and serve with sesame seeds sprinkled as garnish.

Lemon grass

Lemon grass is a type of grass with the same sorts of essential oils found in lemons. Its fragrant aroma is released to its full extent only when during cooking; however, lemon grass is not eaten with the food afterwards. As with spring onions, the soft outer layers are peeled away and only the thick inner portion is used. Lemon grass stays fresh for several weeks when stored in the vegetable compartment of your refrigerator.

VEGETABLE CURRY

■ **Serves 4**

2 peppers
1 bunch scallions
10 oz canned bamboo shoots
7 1/4 oz canned water chestnuts
5–6 tbsp sesame oil
1 lb 5 1/4 oz Chinese vegetable mix
8 3/4 fl oz vegetable stock
3–4 tbsp curry powder
1/2 bunch coriander for garnish

Preparation time:
approx. 20 minutes
362 cal/1523 kJ

Curry

Curry is not available in India and other East Asian countries as a finished product. Instead, curry mixtures are specially prepared according to the needs of each dish. Curry can vary as much in colour as in spiciness. All told, curry can be made from 3 to 15, or more, ground spices.

1 Wash the peppers, remove the pips and cut into slices.

2 Wash the scallions, slice into rings. Place the bamboo shoots and water chestnuts in a strainer and allow to dry well.

3 Heat the oil in the wok and fry the cleaned vegetables together with the vegetable mix for 4–5 minutes, stirring well.

4 Add the vegetable stock and let stew for an additional 8–10 minutes. Stir in the curry powder. Serve garnished with coriander.

BEAN SPROUTS WITH ORANGES

■ **Serves 4**

250 g soybean sprouts
250 g mixed pickles
3–4 tbsp sesame oil
2–3 oranges
smoked tofu
salt
ground pepper
4 tbsp soy sauce
1 bed cress

Preparation time:
approx. 20 minutes
248 cal/1042 kJ

Tofu

Tofu is a type of curd made from soybeans and is one of the staples of the Asian diet. Its high protein content makes it a healthy alternative to meat, and vitamin B1 defends against lethargy and loss of appetite as well. Tofu has very little flavour on its own, and lends itself therefore to many different uses and styles of preparation.

1 Rinse off the soybean sprouts under cold running water. Place in a strainer and allow to dry well. The pickles should also be strained.

2 Heat the oil in the wok and fry the vegetables for a short time, stirring constantly. Peel the oranges in such a way that the white rind is also removed. Separate the wedges with a sharp knife and cut them into small pieces.

3 Cut the tofu into cubes. Add the tofu and the orange slices to the vegetables and season the wok with salt, pepper and soy sauce. Let everything cook for another 2 minutes.

4 Wash and dry the cress, and cut off any roots. Arrange everything in small bowls and serve garnished with cress.

BAKED ENDIVES

■ **Serves 4**

1 lb 1 1/2 oz
endives
8 egg whites
2 egg yolks
salt
2 tbsp meal
1 tbsp cornflour
peanut oil
5 tbsp orange juice
1 tbsp peanut oil
1 tbsp paprika
powder
1 tbsp chilli powder
3/4 oz coriander
5 tbsp soy sauce
1 tbsp five-spice
powder
2–3 tbsp cane
sugar
5 tbsp raspberry
vinegar
1 tbsp sesame oil
1 tbsp sugar
1/4 bunch scallions

Preparation time:
approx. 30 minutes
367 cal/1541 kJ

Five-Spice Powder
The constitution of five-spice powder varies according to country. The recipes are based on fennel seeds, cloves, cardamom or pepper, star anise and cinnamon.

1 Whas the endives, under running water allow them to dry well. Dry the endive leaves and cut them into strips of about 3 inches.

2 Beat the eggs whites until they are stiff. Whisk the egg yolks and mix them with the beaten whites. Add the salt, meal and cornflour. Dip the strips of endive in the mixture and fry them in hot peanut oil until they are brown.

3 For the first sauce, heat the orange juice, remove from the cooker and stir together with peanut oil, paprika power, chilli powder and coriander.

4 For the second sauce, heat the soy sauce and add the five-spice powder together with the sugar. Keep on the cooker, stirring constantly, until the sugar has dissolved.

5 For the third sauce, stir the vinegar together with sesame oil, sugar and salt. Wash the scallions, chop finely and stir into the sauce.

6 Pour the sauces liberally over the endives, arrange and serve.

PAKCHOI WITH EGG

■ Serves 4

1 lb 7–8 oz pakchoi
2 onions
4 whole chillies
3–4 tbsp peanut oil
10 1/2 oz canned
diced tomatoes
4–5 tbsp soy sauce
2–3 tbsp coconut
milk
salt
ground pepper
4–5 cooked quail's
eggs from the jar

Preparation time:
approx. 30 minutes
235 cal/990 kJ

1 Wash and clean the pakchoi, and allow it to dry well. Chop it into bite-sized pieces. Peel the onions and cut into small cubes.

2 Cut the chillies in two, remove the white chamber walls and the pips, and wash the chillies in running water. Cut them into small cubes.

3 Heat the oil in the wok and fry the onion- and chilli-cubes in the oil, stir-ring constantly.

4 Add the pakchoi and onions, cook everything together for a short time, and cover with the diced tomatoes, the soy sauce and the coconut milk. Allow every-thing to braise for approximately 10–15 minutes. Season with salt and pepper.

5 Allow the eggs to dry well, and cut them in two. Arrange the vegetables on a plate and serve garnished with the eggs.

Pakchoi Cabbage

This Chinese rocket salad is reminiscent in its mild aroma of Chinese cabbage. The crunchy white stems and the fresh leaves are tasty raw as a salad or lightly cooked as a vegetable.

SWEET AND SOUR VEGETABLES

■ Serves 4

3 1/2 oz Chinese
cabbage

4 oz carrots

4 oz fresh Shiitake
mushrooms

4 oz snow peas

1 3/4 oz ginger

2 garlic cloves

2 red chillies

3 1/2 oz canned
bamboo shoots

5 1/2 oz pineapple

4 tbsp sunflower
seed oil

4 tbsp rice vinegar

4 tbsp light soy
sauce

4 tbsp sherry

2 tbsp sugar

7 fl oz chicken stock

1 tsp cornflour

Preparation time:
approx. 30 minutes
399 cal/1676 kJ

Soy Sauce

Light soy sauces are saltier and are used with dishes that are not meant to accept any extra colour. In contrast, dark soy sauces have a strong, sweet flavour.

1 Wash the Chinese cabbage, dry it and cut the leaves lengthwise. Then cut them into 2-centimetre-wide strips. Peel the carrots and cut then into thin slices. Rub the mushrooms off with kitchen roll and cut in two.

2 Peel the ginger and cut into very fine slices. Peel the garlic and chop finely. Wash the chillies, remove the pips and cut into slices.

3 Let the bamboo shoots drain in a strainer. Peel the pineapple, remove the stalk and cut the fruit into pieces.

4 Heat the oil in the wok and fry the carrots with the mushrooms, snow peas and Chinese cabbage. Add the ginger, garlic and chilli and fry them quickly for a short time with the rest of the ingredients.

5 Add the bamboo shoots, pineapple, vinegar, soy sauce, sherry and sugar. Pour in three-fourths of the chicken stock and mix in well.

6 Stir the corn flour together with the remaining cold broth, pour over the vegetables and mix immediately. Allow to simmer for 4 minutes. Ladle into bowls and serve.

EGGS WITH MUSHROOMS

■ Serves 4

3 dried morels
3 dried Shiitake mushrooms
1 red chilli pepper
1/4 oz ginger
2 scallions
2 bunches coriander
4 eggs
2 tbsp Soy Sauce
pepper
1 tbsp peanut oil
2 tbsp sunflower seed oil

Preparation time:
approx. 30 minutes
230 cal/966 kJ

1 Place the dried mushrooms in a bowl. Fill the bowl with hot water until the mushrooms are well-covered. Let soak for about 15 minutes.

2 Wash the chillies and remove the pips, and cut them into thin slices. Peel the ginger and chop very finely. Clean the scallions, and cut into rings. Wash the coriander, allow it to dry, and pluck the leaves from the stems.

3 Dry the mushrooms in a strainer and cut into pieces. Whisk the eggs and mix them with the soy sauce, pepper and peanut oil.

4 Heat the sunflower seed oil in the wok. Fry the mushrooms for only a short time, then add the remaining ingredients excepting the egg and coriander, and mix well. Pour in the beaten eggs and cook them until they begin to solidify. Push the solidified egg to the edges of the wok.

5 Serve on pre-warmed plates or bowls, garnished with sprinkled coriander.

Shiitake
The spicy tree fungus, to which exceptional healing properties are attributed, is mainly found, in Europe, dried at the market. Its strong aroma makes it an invaluable spice in soups, sauces and stocks.

31

SZECHUAN CUCUMBERS ON BULGUR

■ Serves 4

2 medium-sized
salad cucumbers
1 bunch scallions
1 ginger root
(2 inches)
2 garlic cloves
1 red chilli pepper
3–4 tbsp sesame
seed oil
1 tbsp cane sugar
2–3 tbsp soy sauce
1–2 tbsp Szechuan
spice
1 tbsp chilli oil
5 1/2 oz bulgur

Preparation time:
approx. 25 minutes
313 cal/1316 kJ

1 Wash the cucumbers, cut into two, remove the pips and cut crosswise into slices. Wash the scallions and slice into fine rings.

2 Peel the garlic and ginger and chop finely. Wash the chilli, remove the pips and chop into small cubes.

3 Heat the oil, and fry the vegetables while stirring for 6–7 minutes. Add the sugar, soy sauce and spice. Pour in the chilli oil as well.

4 Allow everything to simmer for 6–8 minutes. During this time, prepare the bulgur according to the instructions on the packaging. Mix the bulgur carefully with the other ingredients in the wok. Ladle into bowls and serve.

Bulgur
Bulgur is a rich oriental side dish made from cooked, husked and cracked wheat kernels. A type of wheat groat, it is an interesting, protein- and vitamin-rich alternative to rice. When combined with spicy Szechuan cooking, the result is a savoury example of "global cuisine."

SOUR SORREL SOUP

■ Serves 4

14 1/4 oz sour sorrel

5 dried dates

3 1/2 oz canned palm hearts

3–4 tbsp peanut oil

17 1/2 oz vegetable stock

salt

pepper

ginger and nutmeg powder

2–3 tbsp sharp black bean paste

8 3/4 fl oz unsweetened coconut milk

2–3 tbsp sesame seeds

Preparation time: approx. 20 minutes

264 cal/1110 kJ

1 Wash the sorrel, dry and cut coarsely. Mince the dates. Drain the palm hearts and cut into small pieces.

2 Heat the oil in the wok and fry the sorrel along with the dates and the palm hearts for a short time.

3 Pour in the vegetable stock and season with salt, pepper, and ginger- and nutmeg powder. Add the bean paste and let simmer for approximately 10 minutes. Add in the coconut milk and cook for another 1–2 minutes, stirring well.

4 Roast the sesame seeds dry in a pan. Divide the soup into bowls and serve sprinked with the sesame seeds.

Black Bean Paste

Bean paste is a thick spice paste made of fermented soy beans, chilli peppers, garlic and spices. Its consistency can vary from mushy to chunky. You can find bean paste in Asian import shops.

PURE ASIAN: RICE & NOODLES

No dish in Asia is served without rice or noodles! Whether you are preparing a simple, everyday dish or are hoping to put together a sumptuous feast, these basic ingredients, combined with the finest of Asian flavours, are far more than simple side dishes.

RICE WITH PORK FILET

■ **Serves 4**

4–5 oz rice
1 pint 6 oz calf stock
9 fl oz Asia stock
2–3 tbsp soy sauce
2–3 tbsp rice wine
8 3/4 oz gammon filet
1 bunch scallions
2–3 tbsp sesame oil
7 oz green asparagus from the jar
salt, pepper
ginger and garlic powder
1/2 bed cress

Preparation time:
approx. 35 minutes
370 cal/1555 kJ

Rice

Its use in the Chinese language shows how important rice is to Asian culture: to wish someone a happy new year in China, say "May your rice never scorch," and the everyday greeting in Chinese is "Have you eaten rice today?"

1 Place the rice in a strainer and rinse with hot water. Mix the calf stock with the Asia stock, soy sauce and rice wine.

2 Combine the mixture of stocks, soy sauce and rice wine with the rice in a pot and boil. Let simmer over a low heat for 15–20 minutes.

3 Wash and dry the pork filet, and cut it into thin strips. Clean the scallions and cut into rings.

4 Heat the oil in the wok and fry the scallions with the filet for 4–5 minutes, while stirring constantly. Put the asparagus in a strainer and allow it to dry well. Cut the asparagus into bite-sized pieces and put in with the meat. Warm well, and season with the ginger- and garlic powder.

5 Serve the meat and asparagus together with the rice in bowls, and garnish with sprinkled cress.

RICE NOODLES WITH CRAYFISH

■ Serves 4

5 1/4 oz rice-
noodles

1 pint 6 oz lobster
stock

2–3 tbsp ginger
juice

2–3 tbsp soy sauce

a pinch of lemon
pepper

10 1/2 oz crayfish
meat

2 eggs

Preparation time:
approx. 20 minutes
570 cal/2396 kJ

Scrambled Eggs
You can also scramble
the eggs in a separate
pan and break them into
small pieces. Sprinkle
these "egg flakes" over
the noodles before
serving.

1 Soak the noodles in sufficiently warm
water until they are soft. Strain them
well and rinse off with cold water.

2 Heat the lobster stock together with
the ginger juice, soy sauce and lemon
pepper in the wok. Cook the noodles over
a medium heat with the other ingredients
for 3–5 minutes.

3 Add the crayfish meat. Whisk the eggs
and slowly pour into the mixture in the
wok. Allow to set for about a minute over a
low heat, then stir carefully. Ladle the soup
into bowls and serve.

SCENTED RICE WITH FRUIT

■ Serves 4

7 1/4 oz scented or
Basmati rice

7 1/4 oz canned
lychee fruit

2 bananas

1/2 pineapple

1 mango

8 1/4 fl oz
unsweetened
coconut milk

2–3 tbsp sweet
creamed coconut

14–15 fl oz coconut
liqueur

cardamom, clove
and aniseed
powder

1 starfruit

Preparation time:
approx. 30 minutes
348 cal/1464 kJ

Basmati Rice
This rice flourishes,
along with other crops,
in the mountainous
environment of the
Himalayas. It is among
the best of its sort, and
is particularly aromatic
with a fine nutty flavour
and wonderful scent.
The grains stick to one
another after cooking
and the rice is ideal
for eating with a
"chopstick".

1 Prepare the rice according to the packaging instructions. Place the lychees in a strainer and allow to dry well. Afterwards, cut in two.

2 Peel the bananas and cut into slices. Peel the pineapple, remove the stalk and cut the fruit into pieces. Peel the mango, remove the pit and cut the flesh into cubes.

3 Heat the coconut milk slowly in the wok together with the coconut crème and the liqueur. Add the fruit and cook over a low heat for about 4–5minutes.

4 Season until piquant with the cardamom, clove and aniseed. Mix in the well-dried rice. Wash and dry the starfruit, then cut into slices. Arrange the rice on plates, garnish with the starfruit, and serve.

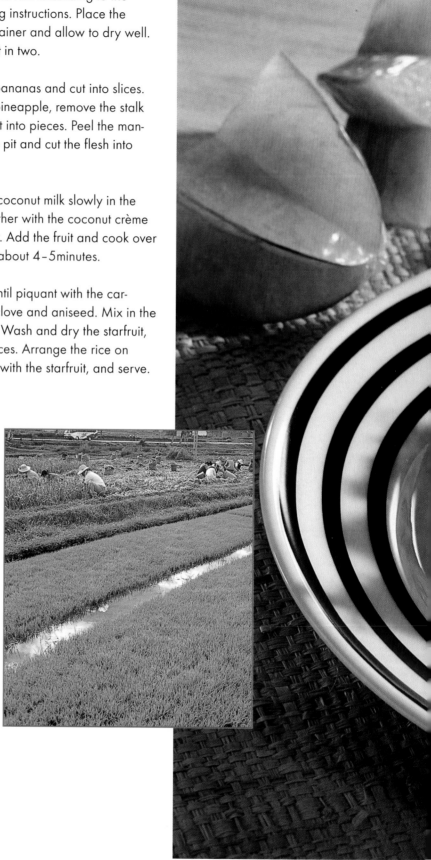

BEAN NOODLES WITH MUSHROOMS

■ Serves 4

3 1/2 oz bean
noodles

1 red, 1 yellow
pepper

3–4 hot chillies

10 1/2 oz oyster
mushrooms

3 garlic cloves

1 fresh ginger root
(1 inch)

6–7 tbsp sesame
seed oil

salt

pepper

mustard seed
powder

1 tbsp chilli sauce

7 tbsp mushroom
stock

Preparation time:
approx. 25 minutes
289 cal/1215 kJ

1 Soak the noodles in warm water until soft. Dry well and cut into pieces of about 3–4 centimetres.

2 Cut the peppers and the chillies in two, remove the seeds and wash. Cut into small cubes.

3 Clean the mushrooms and cut into pieces. Peel the garlic and ginger and chop finely.

4 Heat the oil in the wok and fry the vegetables portion by portion for 3–4 minutes while stirring. Add the noodles and fry for approx. 1 minute, also while stirring.

5 Flavour with the spices, and add the chilli sauce and mushroom stock. Cook over a low heat for another 4–5 minutes. Arrange the noodles with the mushrooms and vegetables, and serve.

Deep-Fried Bean Noodles

If you like noodles firm and stiff, deep-fry these noodles made of mung bean meal. A hint: bean noodles must be soaked in water before being cooked or fried.

YOGHURT RICE WITH LENTILS

■ Serves 4

3 1/2 oz whole-grain rice

1 3/4 oz small green Puy lentils

17 1/2 fl oz vegetable stock

salt

pepper

coriander and ginger powder

2 oz pepper butter

3 1/2 oz pearl onions from the jar

cumin and mustard seed powder

1 tbsp raspberry vinegar

4–5 tbsp organic yoghurt

Preparation time: approx. 30 minutes
298 cal/1253 kJ

Whole-Grain Rice
Shucked, but untreated otherwise, whole-grain rice retains vitamins, fibre and minerals and is therefore quite healthy. The wholesome brown kernels, with their nutty flavour, require a slightly longer preparation time than white rice.

1 Cook the rice together with the lentils and the vegetable stock for approx. 20 minutes. Season with the salt, pepper, coriander and ginger powder.

2 Heat the butter in the wok. Dry the pearl onions well and fry them in the butter while stirring for 4–5 minutes.

3 Strain the rice-lentil mixture. Add to the pearl onions to the wok.

4 Flavour the wok with cumin- and mustard-seed powder. Add the vinegar and cook together for 3–5 minutes over a low heat. Carefully add the yoghurt and serve immediately.

BAMI WITH TUNA FISH

■ **Serves 4**

5 1/4 oz egg stick noodles

10 1/2 oz cherry tomatoes

4 shallots

2 garlic cloves

2 stalks celery

2 carrots

4–5 tbsp chilli oil

salt

pepper

ginger powder

8 3/4 fl oz vegetable stock

2–3 tbsp soy sauce

8 3/4 oz tuna packed in juice

Sambal Oelek

3–4 tbsp roasted onions

Preparation time:
approx. 30 minutes
464 cal/1950 kJ

Tuna Fish

Since sushi has made inroads into European tastes, Europeans know the firm, dark meat raw as well as cooked. Its flavour is reminiscent of calf's meat, and it should always be prepared fresh.

1 Prepare the noodles according to packaging instructions. Wash the tomatoes, cut in two and then in quarters.

2 Peel the shallots and the garlic, and chop into small cubes. Clean the celery and cut into strips.

3 Peel the carrots and cut into strips. Heat the oil in the wok and cook all the vegetables together for 5–6 minutes, stirring often.

4 Season with salt, pepper and ginger powder, and add the vegetable stock and soy sauce. Boil.

5 Dry the tuna and the noodles in a strainer. Carefully add both to the vegetables and cook for about 2–3 minutes.

6 Season the noodles with the Sambal Oelek, arrange with the onions as garnish and serve.

MULTI-COLOURED RICE BOWL

■ Serves 4

1 lb 2 oz rice, salt

For the green rice:
2–3 tbsp sesame oil
3 1/2 oz leaf spinach (frozen)
3 1/2 oz peas
7 tbsp vegetable stock
2–3 tbsp soy sauce
pepper
onion and garlic powder
nutmeg

For the violet rice:
10 1/2 oz red beetroot from the jar
cardamom and mustard seed powder

For the orange rice:
7 1/4 oz sweet and sour canned pumpkin
2 bananas
2–3 canned apricots
2–3 tbsp sesame seed oil
1–2 tbsp yellow curry paste

For the red rice:
10 1/2 oz tomato al gusto with onions and garlic
4–5 tbsp paprika paste
sugar
2–3 tbsp sesame seed oil

Preparation time:
approx. 40 minutes
700 cal/2941 kJ

1 Prepare the rice in boiling salt water according to packaging instructions. Pour out the water and allow the rice to dry well.

2 For the green rice, heat the sesame oil in the wok and quickly fry the coarsely-chopped spinach with the peas. Add the vegetable stock and the soy sauce, and cook over low heat for 3–5 minutes. Season with salt, pepper, onion- and garlic powder and nutmeg, and carefully mix in one quarter of the pre-prepared rice. Remove from the wok and keep warm.

3 For the violet rice, drain the red beetroot well in a strainer, collect the juice that runs off, and cut the beetroot into small cubes. Heat up the beetroot with its juice in the wok. Season with cardamom- and mustard seed powder, and add another quarter of the rice. Remove and keep warm.

4 For the orange rice, strain the pumpkin well. Cut into small cubes. Peel the banana and cut likewise into cubes. Let the apricots dry as well, and chop finely. Heat the sesame oil in the wok and fry the banana, pumpkin and apricot for 1–2 minutes while stirring. Flavour with the curry paste and add a further quarter of the rice. Remove and keep warm.

5 For the red rice, mix the tomato with the paprika paste, salt, pepper and sugar. Heat the sesame oil in the wok and cook the tomato mixture for 1–2 minutes while stirring. Add the rest of the rice and cook. Arrange the four rice colours as balls on plates and serve.

PAD-TAI NOODLES

■ Serves 4

3 1/2 oz flat Thai egg noodles

1 bunch radishes

1 green pepper

7 1/4 oz tofu

2 bunches scallions

4–5 tbsp sesame seed oil

8 3/4 oz scaled fresh shrimp

8 3/4 oz mung bean sprouts

7 tbsp fish oil sauce

3–4 tbsp rice wine

sugar

1 egg

3–4 tbsp chopped, unsalted peanuts

1 natural lemon

Preparation time:
approx. 30 minutes
377 cal/1583 kJ

1 Prepare the noodles according to the packaging instructions. Wash the radishes, dry and cut into slices. Cut the pepper in two, remove the pips and rinse under cold running water. Cut into cubes.

2 Cut the tofu likewise into cubes. Clean the scallions, dry and cut into fine tubes. Heat the oil in the wok and fry the prepared vegetables together with the tofu and the shrimp for 3–4 minutes while stirring.

3 Wash the bean sprouts with warm water, dry well and add to the wok. Douse everything with the fish sauce and the rice wine, and add the well-dried noodles. Flavour with a pinch of sugar and cook for 3–4 minutes over a low heat.

4 Whisk the egg, add to the wok and allow to set over a low heat. Place the noodles onto plates or in bowls, and sprinkle with the peanuts. Cut the lemon into eighths, garnish the noodles with the lemon wedges, and serve.

Thai Noodles
Thai noodles are use predominately for Bami dishes. They are available in a variety of lengths and widths.

NOODLE SOUP WITH CHICKEN

■ Serves 4

4 oz bean sheets or bean curd noodles

17–18 fl oz chicken stock

17–18 fl oz Asia stock

1–2 tbsp Szechuan spice

3 1/2 oz greens (frozen)

14 1/4 oz filet of chicken breast

14 1/4 oz canned straw mushrooms

2–3 tbsp sesame seed oil

salt, pepper coriander powder

1 bunch coriander

Preparation time:
approx. 30 minutes
387 cal/1628 kJ

Bean Sheets

In Asian cuisine, bean sheets are used as an ingredient for soups and stews.

1 Soak the bean sheets in warm water. Then cut into pieces or strips. Bring the chicken and Asian stock to the boil in the wok with the Szechuan spice and the greens.

2 Cook the bean sheets for 15–20 minutes over a low heat in the stock. Wash and dry the chicken filet and cut into small cubes.

3 Strain the straw mushrooms and fry the chicken with the mushrooms for 3–4 minutes, stirring often. Season with salt, pepper and coriander powder.

4 Add everything together in the soup and let simmer for 1–2 minutes. Wash and dry the coriander, and chop finely. Divide the soup into bowls and serve sprinkled with the coriander.

FRIED RICE WITH MEAT BALLS

■ Serves 4

4 red onions,
2 garlic cloves

salt, pepper

4 tbsp butter oil

cinnamon, allspice
and saffron powder

3 1/2 oz round-
grain rice

8 3/4 fl oz Asian
stock

14 1/4 oz gammon

3 1/2 oz onion-gar-
lic mix (frozen)

paprika powder

1 tbsp sharp
mustard

2–3 tbsp almond
leaves

Preparation time:
approx. 30 minutes
683 cal/2869 kJ

Round-Grain Rice
Round-grain rice grains
are almost as thick as
they are long. The rice
has more starch in it as
long-grain rice and after
cooking becomes quite
soft and sticky, making it
well-suited to puddings
and similar dishes.

1 Peel the onions and cut into thin rings. Peel the garlic and press with a small bit of salt. Heat half of the butter oil in the wok and fry the onion rings and the garlic paste until glassy. Add the spices and the rice and cook for 1–2 minutes while stirring.

2 Douse with the Asian stock and cook covered, over a low heat, for 15–20 minutes. Mix the meat with the onion-garlic mix, salt, pepper, paprika powder and mustard. Mould small balls from the mixture.

3 Heat the rest of the butter oil in a pan and fry the meat balls for 4–5 minutes. Add in the meat balls carefully with the rice and fry everything for 4–5 minutes together.

4 Roast the almond leaves dry in a pan until golden brown. Divide the fried rice into bowls with the meat balls and serve garnished with the almond leaves.

DEEP-FRIED GLASS NOODLES

■ Serves 4

14 1/4 oz parsnip
1/2 bunch scallions
10 1/2 oz snow
peas
3–4 tbsp peanut oil
salt, pepper
nutmeg
mustard seed
powder
3–4 tbsp maple
syrup
2–3 tbsp Dijon
mustard
peanut oil for deep-
frying
4 oz glass noodles

Preparation time:
approx. 30 minutes
435 cal/1828 kJ

1 Peel the parsnip and cut into small cubes. Clean the scallions, dry, and cut into 2–5 centimetres long pieces. Clean the snow peas, and allow to dry well.

2 Heat the oil in the wok and fry the vegetables for 3–4 minutes each while stirring. Season with the spices, remove from the wok and allow to drip dry.

3 Stir the maple syrup and the mustard in with the remaining frying oil, and warm carefully. Place the vegetables back in the wok and glaze. Remove and keep warm.

4 Clean the wok and heat enough peanut oil in it to deep-fry with. Fry the glass noodles in the oil until crunchy. Arrange the vegetables with the noodles and serve.

Nutmeg
Its name is misleading, as it is not a nut at all – instead, what we call "nutmeg" is the pollen of the nutmeg tree. Nutmeg, with its sharp, aromatic flavour, originates from the Molucca Islands in Southeast Asia.

MUSHROOMS WITH RICE FILLING

■ **Serves 4**

8 3/4 oz 5-minute rice

10–14 large anise caps

2–3 red onions

3 1/2 oz cooked gammon

3 1/2 oz tomato al gusto with herbs salt, pepper

allspice and coriander powder

4–5 tbsp sesame seed oil

17 1/2 fl oz mushroom stock

1 1/2 oz–3 1/2 oz onion sprouts

1 1/2 oz–3 1/2 oz garden cress

Preparation time: approx. 35 minutes

572 cal/2404 kJ

1 Cook the rice according to packaging instructions. Clean the mushrooms, and allow to dry. Pull off the stems and carefully cut away the gills. Finely chop the mushroom flesh.

2 Peel the onions and cut into fine cubes. Cut the gammon likewise into cubes. Mix the chopped mushrooms with the onion- and gammon cubes and the tomato. Season strongly with salt, pepper, allspice and coriander powder.

3 Heat the oil in the wok and fry the vegetable mix for about 3–4 minutes while stirring constantly. Add the rice, stir well and fill the mushroom caps with the mix.

4 Clean the wok, add in the mushroom stock and bring it to a boil. Put the mushroom caps in a steam basket and put the basket in the wok. Steam the mushrooms in the covered wok for 10–15 minutes over a low heat. Wash the onion sprouts and the garden cress and dry well. Arrange the mushrooms on plates and serve with the onion sprouts and the cress.

Allspice

The flavour of allspice is reminiscent of nutmeg and pepper. The berries are either cooked whole or ground right before use.

"SAIGON" NOODLES

■ Serves 4

8 3/4 oz rice
noodles

2–3 white onions,
4 garlic cloves

2 tbsp canned
ginger

2 tbsp chopped
lemon grass

2–3 tbsp chilli oil

8 3/4 fl oz chicken
stock

3–4 tbsp chilli sauce

2 tbsp soy sauce

2 tbsp Nuoc Nam
(Vietnamese fish
sauce)

2 tbsp brown sugar

1 bunch basil

1–2 tbsp starch
powder

Preparation time:
approx. 20 minutes
377 cal/1586 kJ

Fish Sauce
If you cannot find this
thin sauce made of
salted, fermented fish,
you can use Asian oys-
ter sauce as a substitute.
This somewhat more
expensive sauce is less
heavily salted and has
a stronger aroma.

1 Cook the rice noodles according to packaging instructions. Peel the onions and garlic and chop finely. Place the ginger in a strainer and allow to drip dry. Chop the ginger finely afterwards. Fry the ginger, onion, garlic, and lemon grass in the chilli oil for 2–3 minutes while stirring.

2 Add the chicken stock, chilli sauce, soy sauce, fish sauce and sugar. Simmer for 2–3 minutes over a low heat.

3 Wash and dry the basil and cut into fine strips. Add to the sauce and cook for 1–2 minutes. Stir the starch powder with water until smooth, and use to thicken the sauce.

4 Divide the noodles onto plates, and serve with the sauce.

RICE-CHICKPEA PILAF

■ Serves 4

3–4 tbsp sesame
seed oil

3 1/2 oz round-
grain rice

cumin, cinnamon,
nutmeg and allspice
powder

salt, pepper

17 1/2 tbsp lamb
stock

7 tbsp light port
wine

12 1/4 oz canned
chickpeas

1/2 bunch
coriander

Preparation time:
approx. 35 minutes
413 cal/1735 kJ

Chickpeas
In India, many Middle
Eastern countries and in
Mexico, the chickpea,
with its nutty flavour, is a
staple food and is also
ground into meal. If
roasted in a pan with
only a small amount of
oil, chickpeas become
crunchy like nuts.

1 Heat the sesame seed oil in the wok
and fry the round-grain rice for 3–4
minutes, or until light brown and glazed.
Stir often.

2 Season the rice strongly with the spices
and douse with the lamb stock and
port wine. Cook covered over a low heat
for 15–20 minutes, until the moisture has
been absorbed. Put the chickpeas in a
strainer and allow them to drip dry.

3 Mix the chickpeas with the rice in the
wok and heat for 2–3 minutes. Wash
and dry the coriander, pluck the leaves and
chop finely. Divide the rice onto plates and
serve garnished with the coriander.

SPICY FOWL

The internationally-known Peking duck is arguably the epitome of Asian fowl cooking — but we'll show you here that Asian cuisine offers much, much more. Try our wok recipes for chicken, turkey, duck, guinea fowl, goose or pheasant, baked, braised or marinated with yoghurt and spices.

CHICKEN IN GINGER WINE

■ **Serves 4**

14 1/4 oz filet of chicken breast

1 fresh ginger root (2 inches)

3 garlic cloves

3–4 tbsp sesame seed oil

salt

pepper

ginger and coriander powder

3 tbsp spice ketchup

14 1/4 fl oz dry sherry

7 1/4 fl oz plum schnapps

1/2 bunch coriander

Tabasco sauce

Preparation time:
approx. 20 minutes
397 cal/1668 kJ

Ginger

The most important spice in Asian cooking, ginger gives off its best aroma when the root is grated fresh. When shopping for ginger, make sure that the root is quite firm and glossy, and when scraped with a finger-nail, it should make a squeaking noise.

1 Wash and dry the chicken breast filet, and cut into small slices. Peel the ginger and grate finely. Peel the garlic and cut it into fine cubes.

2 Heat the oil in the wok and fry the chicken, together with the ginger and the garlic cubes, for 5–6 minutes while stirring constantly. Season with salt, pepper, and ginger and coriander powder.

3 Add the ketchup, sherry and plum schnapps to the wok and cook for an additional 3–5 minutes over a low heat. Wash and dry the coriander and pluck the leaves.

4 Top off the flavour of the chicken with Tabasco, and serve garnished with coriander. This dish goes very well with prawn crackers.

TURKEY RAGOUT WITH COCONU

■ Serves 4

1 lb 5–6 oz filet of turkey breast
1 red pepper
8 3/4 oz scallions
1 bunch basil
14 1/4 fl oz unsweetened coconut milk
1 tbsp red curry paste
2 tbsp soy sauce
1 tbsp sugar

Preparation time:
approx. 20 minutes
290 cal/1221 kJ

1 Wash and dry the turkey breast, then cut into slices. Wash the pepper and cut into two; remove the pips and cut likewise into slices.

2 Wash and clean the scallions and cut into pieces of approximately 5 centimetres. Wash and dry the basil; pull the leaves from the stalks and chop one-half into fine flakes. Set aside the other half for decoration.

3 Boil the coconut milk in the wok, add in the turkey meat and the curry paste and stir everything together. Let simmer for about 1 minute. Stir occasionally.

4 Add the vegetables and let simmer for an additional 3 minutes. Add the chopped basil, the soy sauce and the sugar to taste.

5 Arrange the turkey ragout on plates and serve garnished with the rest of the basil.

Curry Paste

Curry pastes – red, yellow and green – are no longer a stranger to the cuisine of South-east Asia. In Thailand especially, most dishes are based on this mixture of chilli, garlic, onions, soy oil and prawn paste. While the red paste goes with red vegetables and meat, the green paste is used for green vegetables and the yellow for fish and fowl.

SPICY DRUMSTICKS

■ Serves 4

12–14 drumsticks, precooked

1/2 tbsp salt

1 tbsp five-spice powder

2 tbsp light soy sauce

1 tbsp dark soy sauce

2 tbsp rice wine

2 tbsp sesame seed oil

3 scallions

1 fresh ginger root (2 inches)

2 eggs

3 1/2 oz cornflakes

1 tbsp corn flour

peanut oil for deep frying

Hoisin sauce

Preparation time: approx. 35 minutes
990 cal/4159 kJ

Scallions

The fresh and mild flavour of scallions is also valued quite highly in Asian cuisine. Its possibilities for use are many: it is good raw in a salad as well as, after a short cooking time, a vegetable or accompaniment for fowl.

1 Wash and dry the drumsticks, and pierce each several times with a pointed knife.

2 Mix the salt with the five-spice powder, the soy sauce, the rice wine and the oil. Clean the scallions, and chop finely. Peel the ginger and grate finely.

3 Add the ginger and the scallions to the marinade. Baste the drumsticks with the marinade and let marinate for about 20 minutes.

4 Whisk the eggs. Crush the cornflakes. Dab off the drumsticks with kitchen roll and dip in the egg. Powder with corn flour and coat with the cornflakes.

5 Heat the oil in the wok and deep-fry the drumsticks for 3–5 minutes. Serve with the Hoisin sauce.

GUINEA FOWL WITH BROCCOLI

■ Serves 4

14 1/4 oz skinless
guinea fowl breast
and bones

3–4 tbsp peanut oil

7 1/4 oz Mung
bean sprouts

7 1/4 oz broccoli
(frozen)

salt

pepper

freshly-grated
nutmeg

cumin

1–2 tbsp chicken
stock

1 tbsp corn flour

1 tbsp hulled
sesame seeds

Preparation time:
approx. 20 minutes
339 cal/1423 kJ

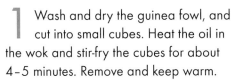

Broccoli

The ancestor of the cau-
liflower, with its typically
nutty flavour, is even
healthier than its relative;
broccoli contains much
more carotene and
about twice as much
vitamin C, iron and
potassium. When shop-
ping for broccoli, watch
that it is fresh and has
no limp leaves.

1 Wash and dry the guinea fowl, and cut into small cubes. Heat the oil in the wok and stir-fry the cubes for about 4–5 minutes. Remove and keep warm.

2 Wash the sprouts, place into a strainer and allow to drain. Fry together with the broccoli in the remaining oil for 3–5 minutes. Season with salt, pepper, nutmeg and cumin, and place the meat once more into the wok.

3 Stir the chicken stock together with the corn flour and mix into the wok. Roast the sesame seeds dry in another pan.

4 Arrange the guinea fowl with the broccoli and sprouts on plates and sprinkle with the sesame seeds. Serve.

CRISPY DUCK WITH PINEAPPLE

■ **Serves 4**

7–7 1/2 oz whole grain meal
1 tbsp walnut oil
4–5 tbsp milk
2–3 eggs
salt
7 tbsp port wine
5 tbsp grated coconut
2 baby pineapples
1 lb 12 oz duck breast filet
peanut oil for deep-frying
5 1/4 oz canned mandarins
5 1/4 oz sweet and sour canned ginger
2–3 tbsp ketchup
coriander, nutmeg and aniseed powder
cayenne pepper
5 1/4 oz mayonnaise
3 1/2 oz yoghurt
1 small apple
1 banana
2 tbsp curry powder
1 tbsp chopped almonds
1 tbsp maple syrup
1/2 bunch lemon balm
1 whole lemon

Preparation time:
approx. 30 minutes
1394 cal/5869 kJ

1 Stir the oil, milk, eggs, salt, port wine and the coconut slivers into a smooth dough. Peel the baby pineapples, cut into quarters and remove the stalks.

2 Wash and dry the breast filets, and cut into cubes. Heat sufficient oil for deep-frying in the wok. Dip the cubes of meat and the pineapple chunks in the dough and fry for 6–8 minutes portion by portion. Remove, dab dry with kitchen roll and keep warm.

3 For the red dip, drain the mandarins and the ginger in a strainer. Puree together with the ketchup, coriander, nutmeg, aniseed and cayenne with the sharp blade of the hand beater.

4 For the yellow dip, stir the mayonnaise together with the yoghurt until smooth. Peel the apple and banana and cut into small cubes. Stir into the mayonnaise-yoghurt mixture together with the curry powder, the almonds and the maple syrup. Add salt to season.

5 Wash and dry the lemon balm, and pluck the leaves. Wash the lemon and cut into wedges. Arrange both dips together with the meat- and pineapple cubes. Garnish with the lemon wedges and lemon balm, and serve.

MINI POULTRY ROLLS

■ Serves 4

10 1/2 oz turkey cutlet

7 1/4 oz Surumi (imitation crab meat)

3 slices cooked ham

1–2 tbsp sharp mustard

3–4 tbsp peanut oil

salt

cayenne pepper

allspice powder

7 tbsp Asia stock

2–3 tbsp Mirin (sweet rice wine)

2–3 tbsp light soy sauce

1 tbsp cornflour

Preparation time:
approx. 20 minutes
257 cal/1082 kJ

1 Wash and dry the cutlet, cut in half and pound the meat until it is quite thin. Chop the Surumi and the cooked ham finely.

2 Wash the coriander, dry it and likewise chop it finely. Afterwards mix in with the Surumi and the ham.

3 Stripe the slices of turkey meat with mustard, and spread the Surumi mixture on as well. Roll the slices, and hold them fast with toothpicks.

4 Heat the oil in the wok and fry the rolls on all sides. Season with salt, cayenne pepper and allspice powder, and pour in the stock. Braise for 6–7 minutes over a low heat.

5 Clean the scallions, and cut into fine rings. Mix with the Mirin wine and add to the wok; cook for another 3–4 minutes.

6 Mix the soy sauce together with the cornflour and stir into the wok. Serve the rolls together with the sauce. This dish goes well with Mie noodles.

Surumi

Surumi is fish-protein paste from Japan, artificially flavoured like crab meat. You can find it in the store labelled as "crabmeat" in the form of skewers, morsels, lobster tails, crab claws, etc. This "crabmeat" is highly recommended, as it is equal in quality but much less costly than the actual crustacean.

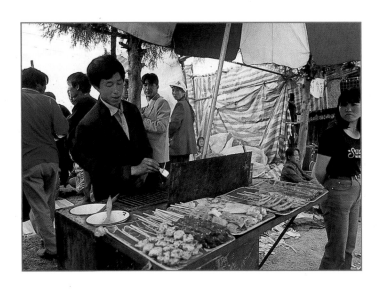

SAVOURY CHICKEN LEGS

■ Serves 4

4 chicken legs (each approx. 7 oz)
7 oz "Prince" mushrooms
3 1/2 oz fennel
3 1/2 oz snow peas
3 1/2 oz parsnip
salt, pepper
paprika powder
mustard seed powder
2–3 tbsp peanut or sesame seed oil

Preparation time:
approx. 30 minutes
625 cal/2625 kJ

Bamboo Steam Basket

This Chinese vessel is available in shops specialising in Asian imports. Before use, it should always be well-soaked in water. The basket, filled with ingredients, is placed in the wok above boiling water or stock. However, there cannot be so much liquid in the wok that the bottom of the basket gets wet. Always close the basket well with a lid or a hand towel.

1 Wash and dry the chicken legs, and carve the skin crosswise. Clean the mushrooms and cut into slices.

2 Clean, wash and slice the fennel. Lay the green aside for garnish.

3 Wash the sugar peas and remove their tips. Peel the parsnip and cut into slices.

4 Brush the chicken legs with the spices and fry in the oil on all sides.

5 Place the vegetables in a bamboo steam basket. Lay the chicken on top and steam everything in the wok for 15–20 minutes.

6 Arrange the chicken with the vegetables, and serve garnished with fennel.

PHEASANT BREAST WITH OKRA

■ Serves 4

14 1/4 oz boneless
pheasant breast

salt

cayenne pepper

cumin

coriander powder

paprika powder

4–5 tbsp sesame
seed oil

10 1/2 oz canned
okra shoots

2 shallots

2 garlic cloves

1 fresh ginger root
(1–2 inches)

7 1/4 oz canned
diced tomatoes

8 3/4 oz unsweet-
ened coconut milk

1/2 bunch
coriander

Preparation time:
approx. 25 minutes
538 cal/2259 kJ

1 Wash the pheasant breast, dry and cut into thin strips. Rub the meat with the spice powders.

2 Heat the oil in the wok and fry the strips of flesh well. Remove and keep warm.

3 Drain the okra well in a strainer. Cut into rings afterwards. Peel the shallots, garlic and ginger and chop finely.

4 Fry the vegetables in the remaining oil for 3–4 minutes, stirring constantly.

5 Add the meat, tomatoes and coconut milk and braise together for an additional 3–4 minutes over low heat. Remove, and serve garnished with coriander.

Okra Shoots

The oblong, mildly spicy okras are the unripe fruit of the rose poplar. They can be prepared in many ways and are excellent raw as a salad, cooked as a side dish or used for an appetizer.

STEWED TURKEY LEGS

■ **Serves 4**

2 lb 2 oz turkey legs

4 tbsp Tandoori paste

1 bunch scallions

2–3 tbsp peanut oil

8 3/4 fl oz poultry stock

7 1/4 fl oz coconut milk

4 tbsp soy sauce

14 1/4 oz Chinese mixed vegetables (frozen)

2 roasted Nori leaves

Preparation time: approx. 50 minutes
570 cal/2394 kJ

1 Wash and dry the meat and cut into cubes. Coat with the Tandoori-paste and allow to set for approximately 20 minutes.

2 Clean the scallions. Cut into small rings.

3 Heat the oil in the wok and fry the meat on all sides for 6–7 minutes.

4 Pour in the poultry stock and the coconut milk and stew for 20–25 minutes. If desired, add a small amount of soy sauce.

5 10 minutes before the end of the cooking time, add the vegetables and the scallions and stew them with the rest of the ingredients. Place the meat with the sauce onto plates, crumble the Nori leaves and sprinkle them across the meat. Serve with colored prawn crackers.

Nori Leaves
Dried seaweed in the form of pressed and dried Nori leaves is the Japanese way of adding seasoning. The ocean-derived vegetable is most well known as the outer casing for sushi. Crumbled, though, it is also used as seasoning for rice, noodle and poultry dishes.

GUINEA FOWL APPETIZER

■ Serves 4

1 lb 5–6 oz filet of
guinea fowl breast

3–4 tbsp lemon
pepper

5 1/4 oz chickpea
flour

2–3 tsp oil

1 tsp ground cumin

1/4 tsp ground
coriander

1/4 tsp cayenne
pepper

salt

peanut oil for
deep-frying

1 bunch mint

7 oz yoghurt

2 tbsp double
cream

Aalspice, garlic and
mustard seed
powder

pepper

1/2 head lollo rosso

Preparation time:
approx. 30 minutes
716 cal/3010 kJ

1 Wash and dry the meat, and cut into thin strips. Season the strips with lemon pepper and let set for 10–15 minutes.

2 Stir the flour together with the oil, the spices and 3 tbsp water. Heat a sufficient amount of peanut oil in the wok. Dip the meat portion by portion in the batter and fry in hot oil until golden brown.

3 Wash and dry the herbs, and chop finely. Stir the yoghurt together with the double cream until smooth.

4 Add the herbs to the wok and flavour with allspice, garlic and mustard seed powder, and salt and pepper.

5 Wash and dry the lollo rosso and cover a large platter with the leaves. Spoon the yoghurt dip into small bowls and set in the middle of the platter. Arrange the strips of meat around the bowls, and serve.

Lemon Balm

Lemon balm is a fresh cooking herb that smells and tastes like lemon. It is used to season sauces, salads, poultry, vegetables and fish and lends to the dishes an Eastern touch. Lemon balm should not be cooked with the dishes it flavours.

THAI POULTRY CURRY

■ Serves 4

14 1/4 oz skinless and boneless turkey breast

3 1/2 oz champignons

3 1/2 oz canned bamboo shoots

1 bunch scallions

3–4 tbsp sesame seed oil

3 1/2 oz peas (frozen)

1 tbsp red curry paste

2 tbsp fish sauce

1–2 tbsp soy sauce

1 tbsp lemon juice

8 3/4 oz unsweetened coconut milk

1/2 bunch coriander

coriander, garlic and ginger powder

Preparation time: approx. 20 minutes
213 cal/897 kJ

Coconut Milk

The slightly sweet mixture of warm water or milk and finely-grated coconut is especially good for adding flavour to sauces, meats and poultry dishes.

1 Wash and dry the turkey breast and cut into fine cubes. Clean the champignons and cut them into small pieces.

2 Drain the bamboo shoots well in a strainer. Clean the scallions and cut into small rings.

3 Heat the oil in the wok and fry the cubed meat for 3–4 minutes. Add the vegetables and the peas and fry for another 1–2 minutes.

4 Stir the curry paste together with the fish sauce, the soy sauce the lemon juice and the coconut milk. Add to the wok and cook everything together for 2–3 minutes over a low heat. Wash and dry the coriander, and chop the leaves well.

5 Season the curry well with the coriander, garlic and ginger powder, divide onto plates and serve garnished with coriander.

SPICY DUCK SOUP

■ Serves 4

14 oz duck legs or
the remains of a
roast duck

1–2 tbsp peanut oil

3 red chilli peppers

3 garlic cloves

3 shallots

3 tbsp fish sauce

3 1/2 oz oyster
mushrooms

2–3 tbsp chilli sauce

17 1/2 fl oz
coconut milk

17 1/2 fl oz
duck stock

1/2 bunch Thai
basil

Preparation time:
approx. 25 minutes
553 cal/2325 kJ

Thai Basil
Thai basil has almost
nothing in common
with the variety of basil
known to us.
The stiffer leaves of the
Thai basil have a bitter
flavour and are
reminiscent of aniseed.

1 Remove the bones and the skin from the duck legs, and cut the meat into small bits.

2 Heat the oil in the wok and fry the meat well. Remove and keep warm.

3 Cut the chillies in two, removing the pips. Wash under cold running water and cut into strips.

4 Peel the garlic and the shallots, and cut into slices.

5 Stir the chillies, garlic and shallots together with the fish sauce, and fry in the leftover oil for 3–4 minutes while stirring.

6 Clean the oyster mushrooms, slice finely and add to the wok. Pour the chilli sauce, coconut milk and duck stock in as well, and put the meat back in again. Cook over a low heat for 6–7 minutes.

7 Wash and dry the basil, and cut into thin strips. Add to the wok and cook for an additional 2 minutes. Ladle the soup into bowls and serve.

GOOSE BREAST WITH CHICKPEAS

■ **Serves 4**

10–11 oz canned chickpeas
7 1/4 oz alfalfa sprouts
1 bunch scallions
3 1/2 oz canned sweetcorn
3–4 tbsp chilli oil
1/2 bunch savoury
7 tbsp malt beer
coriander, nutmeg and mustard seed powder
14 oz smoked goose breast

Preparation time:
approx. 20 minutes
459 cal/1930 kJ

1 Place the chickpeas in a strainer and let drip dry. Wash and dry the alfalfa sprouts.

2 Clean the scallions, and cut into fine tubes. Drain the sweetcorn in a strainer as well.

3 Heat the oil in the wok and fry the vegetables for 4–5 minutes while stirring.

4 Wash and dry the savoury, and pluck the leaves. Add with the malt beer to the chickpeas and cook everything for 4–5 minutes over a low heat.

5 Season the vegetables with coriander, nutmeg and mustard seed powder. Cut the goose breast into thin strips and serve with the chickpeas and alfalfa.

Alfalfa Sprouts

Alfalfa sprouts are the thin sprouts of the Lucerne plant. When fresh, they posses a slightly bitter, cress-like flavour with a hint of nuts. The "queen of sprouts" is moreover rich in trace elements, minerals, vitamin C and plant protein.

SPRING ROLLS

■ **Serves 4**

7 1/4 oz filet of chicken breast

3 1/2 oz bean sprouts

3 1/2 oz Chinese cabbage

3 1/2 oz cooked ham

3 1/2 oz canned champignons

salt, pepper

coriander, ginger and garlic powder

2–3 tbsp soy sauce

4–5 tbsp peanut oil

12–15 spring roll coverings or rice batter leaves

1 egg white

oil for deep frying

Hoisin sauce and

sweet and sour sauce, both for dipping

Preparation time: approx. 30 minutes 402 cal/1691 kJ

1 Wash and dry the filet, and chop into small bits. Wash the bean sprouts and allow to drip dry.

2 Wash the Chinese cabbage and cut into fine strips. Chop the ham into small cubes. Drain the champignons well in a strainer. Mix everything together with the spices and the soy sauce.

3 Heat the oil in the wok and fry the ingredients for 4–5 minutes while stirring.

4 Spread the coverings over a work surface. Spread filling in the middle of each. Prepare the spring rolls according to the packaging instructions.

5 Heat a sufficient amount of oil in the wok and deep fry the spring rolls until golden brown. Let dry on kitchen roll and serve with the Hoisin- and sweet and sour sauce.

Rice Batter Leaves

You can almost always find these porous noodle-batter discs for spring rolls in Asian import shops or in well-stocked specialty stores. They can be used without any further preparation. Transparent rice paper, which can also be used for spring rolls, must first be soaked until soft.

CHICKEN FILET WITH TOFU

■ **Serves 4**

10 1/2 oz filet of chicken breast

2 shallots

3 1/2 oz canned pumpkin

3 1/2 oz canned sweetcorn

3 1/2 oz canned celery

2–3 tbsp sesame seed oil

3–4 tbsp Hoisin sauce

3–4 tbsp rice wine

3 1/2 oz tofu

five-spice powder

Preparation time: approx. 40 minutes
324 cal/1363

Pumpkin

Canned or fresh, pumpkin is an interesting vegetable that lends itself well to cooking. Whether from musk-, spaghetti-, garden- melon pumpkin, the appetising yellow-to-orange flesh with its light, unmistakable flavour goes well with Oriental and Asian cuisine.

1 Wash and dry the chicken filet, and cut into fine strips. Peel the shallots and chop into small cubes.

2 Drain the pumpkin, sweetcorn and celery in a strainer. Cut everything into small strips. Mix the chicken meat with the vegetables.

3 Mix the oil with the Hoisin sauce and the rice wine, pour over the meat-vegetable mix and let marinate for approximately 15 minutes. Afterwards, stew in the wok with the marinade for 8–10 minutes.

4 Cube the tofu and add carefully to the wok. Season well with the five-spice powder and serve in bowls.

POULTRY LEAVES

■ Serves 4

3 shallots

2–3 stalks marjoram

7 1/4 oz chicken liver (or other poultry)

10 1/2 oz boneless, skinless breast of wild duck

2 tbsp rice wine

2 tbsp soy sauce

3 1/2 oz raisins

1 tbsp lemon pepper

1/2 tbsp each of nutmeg, aniseed and ginger powder

3–4 tbsp sesame seed oil

8–10 small savoy leaves

17 1/2 fl oz poultry stock

8 3/4 fl oz port wine

5 tbsp chicken stock

5 tbsp mango juice

4 tbsp tomato ketchup

1 tsp chilli oil

salt

1 tsp sugar

1 tbsp cornflour

Preparation time: approx. 45 minutes
481 cal/2020 kJ

1 Peel and finely cube the shallots. Wash and dry the marjoram, and pluck the leaves from the stalks.

2 Wash and dry the liver and the duck breast, and cut into small cubes.

3 Mix the soy sauce with the rice wine, raisins, lemon pepper and the spices. Immerse the shallot cubes along with the marjoram leaves and the meat in the mixture let marinate for 10–15 minutes.

4 Heat the oil in the wok and fry the mixture for 3–5 minutes while stirring. Remove and let cool.

5 Wash the savoy, blanche quickly in boiling water, rinse in cold water, drip dry well and spread on a work surface.

6 Divide the meat-vegetable mix onto the savoy leaves and clasp the leaves into small packets. Fasten with cooking wire and place in a bamboo basket

7 Mix the poultry stock with the port wine and bring to the boil in the wok. Place the bamboo basket with the savoy packets in the wok. Steam for 10–15 minutes.

8 In the meantime, stir the chicken stock together with the mango juice, ketchup, oil, salt, sugar and cornflour. Bring the mixture to the boil while stirring. Arrange the packets with the sauce and serve.

ROMAINE HEARTS

■ Serves 4

14 1/4 oz turkey filet

10 sage leaves

4 tbsp roasted peanuts

3–4 tbsp peanut oil

1/2–1 tbsp sharp bean paste

3–4 heads mini Romaine lettuce

3 1/2 oz canned pearl onions

8–9 fl oz Asia stock

3 1/2 oz glass noodles

Preparation time: approx. 20 minutes
351 cal/1475 kJ

1 Wash and dry the filet, and cut into fine strips. Wash and dry the sage and chop finely. Chop the peanuts as well.

2 Heat the oil in the wok and fry the prepared ingredients for 3–4 minutes while stirring. Add the bean paste and cook for 1 additional minute while stirring.

3 Wash and dry the heads of lettuce, then cut into quarters. Let the pearl onions drip dry in a strainer.

4 Add the onions to the wok and stir for 1–2 minutes. Bring the stock to the boil, pour over the glass noodles and let rest for 1–2 minutes.

5 Add the noodles and stock into the wok and cook for another 1–2 minutes. Place the salad hearts on plates and divide the sauce with the meat over the lettuce. Serve.

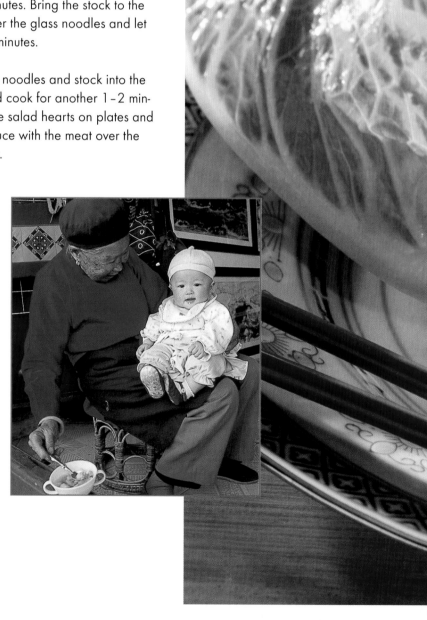

Glass Noodles

Glass noodles are nearly-transparent noodles made of mung bean flour. They are not cooked, instead they are soaked in water and doused in hot liquid. Their gelatine-like consistency makes them an ideal ingredient in soups. When deep-fried, they turn into crunchy shapes of feather-light weight.

DUCK LEGS WITH VEGETABLES

■ Serves 4

4 duck legs

salt

pepper

**3 1/2 oz greens
(frozen)**

**17 1/2 fl oz Asia
stock**

**2–3 tbsp sesame
seed oil**

2 tbsp soy sauce

**14 1/4 oz mixed-
vegetables (frozen)**

Plum sauce

Preparation time:
approx. 30 minutes
442 cal/1858 kJ

1 Wash and dry the duck meat. Rub with salt and pepper.

2 Bring the Asia stock with the greens to a boil in the wok. Add the legs and cook over a low heat for approximately 10 minutes. Remove the meat and let drip dry.

3 Heat the oil in the wok and fry the meat on all sides for 4–5 minutes. Add the soy sauce and let braise for another 2–3 minutes. Remove and keep warm.

4 Add the vegetables into the wok and fry for 6–8 minutes. Arrange the legs over the vegetables and serve with the plum sauce.

Plum Sauce

Plum sauce is a sweet-savoury mix made of
puréed plums, sugar, vinegar and garlic. The
sauce is especially favoured in Asian cuisine
for duck dishes (i.e. Peking duck) and goes
well as a dip for hearty cold dishes. You can
find plum sauce in well-stocked specialty
stores or Asian import shops.

SPICY MEAT & GAME

Spicy or sweet and sour, the particular preparation of meat in the wok promises meat-lovers the greatest of pleasures. Wild game, pork and beef become crispy on the outside, yet stay juicy within.

BRAISED SHOULDER

■ Serves 4

1 lb 5–6 oz pork
shoulder

3–4 tbsp sesame
seed oil

3 tbsp sherry
vinegar

6 tbsp soy sauce

4 tbsp honey

1 tbsp five-spice
powder

5–9 fl oz beeff stock

3 1/2 oz greens
(frozen)

3 1/2 oz canned
pearl onions

1 tsp cornflour

mango chutney for
serving

Preparation time:
approx. 35 minutes
674 cal/2830 kJ

Pork Shoulder

The shoulder is a hearty
and inexpensive piece
of meat. Cut into small
bits, it can be prepared
quickly and succulently.

1 Wash and dry the meat, and cut into
small bits. Heat the oil in the wok and
fry the meat for 4–5 minutes.

2 Mix the vinegar together with the soy
sauce, the honey, the five-spice powder and the beef stock. Add all to the wok
and braise for 15–20 minutes while stirring.

3 After a while, add a bit of soy sauce.
Remove the meat and keep warm. Stir
the cornflour together with a small amount
of cold water, and use this mixture to thick-
en the stock.

4 Arrange the vegetables together with
the meat and the mango chutney, and
serve.

SPICY SOUR DEER

■ Serves 4

1 lb 6 oz deer
gulash meat

3–4 tbsp raspberry
vinegar

4–5 tbsp red wine

1 tsp spicy Chinese
mustard

5–6 tbsp sesame
seed oil

salt

pepper

nutmeg, aniseed
and cardamom
powder

10 1/2 oz jarred
red beet strips

7 1/4 oz red onions

Preparation time:
approx. 40 minutes
350 cal/1573 kJ

1 Cut the gulash into smaller bits if desired. Mix the vinegar with the red
wine, the mustard, the oil and the spices,
mix with the meat and let marinate for
10–15 minutes.

2 Heat the wok and fry the meat with
the marinade for 10–15 minutes while
stirring.

3 Drain the red beet in a strainer. Peel
the onions and cut into rings.

4 Add both the beet and the onions to
the gulash five minutes before the end
of the preparation time. Arrange the gulash
with wild rice and serve.

**Deer or Game
Gulash**

Deer or wild game
gulash is available
throughout the year in
good quality as a frozen
product. Wild game
can be an interesting
alternative choice for
cooking in the wok.

ASIAN HAM

■ Serves 4

1 lb 10 1/2 oz ham
filet
1 3/4 oz ginger
4 garlic cloves
3 red chillies
5 tomatoes
1 pineapple
2 tbsp sesame
seed oil
2 tbsp sunflower
seed oil
4 tbsp rice vinegar
4 tbsp soy sauce
14–15 fl oz sherry
2 tbsp sugar
9 fl oz chicken stock
2 tsp cornflour

Preparation time:
approx. 30 minutes
508 cal/2133 kJ

1 Wash and dry the meat and cut into equally-sized strips. Peel the ginger and cut into very fine slices. Peel and press the garlic.

2 Wash the chillies, cut in two, remove the pips and cut into slices. Wash the tomatoes, cut them crosswise, dip quickly in boiling water, rinse in cold water and peel. Afterwards cut into cubes.

3 Peel the pineapple, remove the stem and cut the flesh into bits. Heat the sesame- and sunflower oil in the wok and fry the meat.

4 Add the ginger, garlic and chillies to the wok. Stir in the tomatoes and the pineapple as well, and fry for a short time.

5 Add the vinegar, soy sauce, sherry and sugar. Pour in 3/4 of the stock and allow everything to cook for another 3 minutes.

6 Mix the cornflour with the remaining 1/4 of the stock, then add in equal portions to the meat. Allow to cook for another 3 minutes. Afterwards, ladle into bowls and serve.

Ginger
In order to make the most of ginger's unique, sharp aroma, it should always be cooked with the dish in question. Besides being used as a delicate spice, ginger can also be candied and coated with chocolate, or made into ginger pralines.

BEEF STIR-FRY

■ **Serves 4**

1 lb 6 oz Join steak
2–3 tbsp soy sauce
1 tbsp chilli oil
1 tsp sugar
1 tbsp freshly-grated ginger
14 fl oz aniseed schnapps
lemon pepper
cumin powder
mustard seed powder
3–4 tbsp peanut oil
5–6 oz canned straw mushrooms
3 1/2 oz canned waterchestnuts
2 red chillies

Preparation time: approx. 30 minutes
328 cal/1379 kJ

1 Wash and dry the meat, and cut into thin strips.

2 Mix the soy sauce with the chilli oil, sugar, ginger, schnapps and the spices. Marinate the meat for 10–15 minutes in the mixture.

3 Heat half the peanut oil in the wok and fry the meat for 3–4 minutes while stirring.

4 Drain the mushrooms and waterchestnuts in a strainer. Afterwards cut each in two. Cut the chillies in two and wash them under running water. Remove the pips. Cut into rings.

5 Heat the rest of the peanut oil in the wok and fry the vegetables for approximately 2 minutes, stirring well. Add the meat and stir-fry everything for another 1–2 minutes. Arrange the spicy beef strips on a plate and serve. Chinese noodles are a good side dish.

Straw Mushrooms

Straw mushrooms are round, cultivated Chinese mushrooms with a grey-black cap and cream-coloured gills. They have a delicate aroma and are ideally suited to seasoning Asian dishes. They can be found canned in Asian import stores or in specialty shops.

SPICY CURRY

■ Serves 4

1 lb 6 oz gammon on the bone

5–6 tbsp sesame seed oil

3 1/2 oz onion-garlic mix (frozen)

7 tbsp vegetable stock

1 tbsp plum sauce

2 tbsp green curry paste

1–2 tbsp pine seeds

Preparation time:
approx. 20 minutes
360 cal/1513 kJ

Pine Seeds
Pine seeds are the edible, oily seeds of the pine tree. Their creamy texture has a flavour reminiscent of almonds. Roasted, they are especially good for meat- and seafood dishes, dips and desserts.

1 Wash and dry the meat, and cut into fine cubes. Heat the oil in the wok and fry the meat well while stirring. Remove and keep warm.

2 Add the onion-garlic mix, the vegetable stock, the plum sauce and the curry paste to the remaining oil and simmer for 2–3 minutes over a low heat.

3 Add the meat and braise for 6–7 minutes. Roast the pine seeds dry in a pan. Dish the curry and serve sprinkled with the roasted pine seeds. Basmati rice makes a good side dish.

FILLED MEAT ROLLS

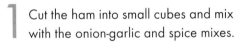

■ **Serves 4**

3 1/2 oz cooked ham

3 1/2 oz onion-garlic mix (frozen)

3 1/2 oz 8-spice mix (frozen)

3 1/2 oz Shiitake mushrooms

3 1/2 oz feta cheese

2–3 tbsp sesame seed oil

salt

pepper

14–15 oz very thin veal or pork cutlets

2–3 tbsp creamed horseradish

4–5 tbsp peanut oil

9–17 fl oz Asia stock

Hoisin sauce for serving

Preparation time:
approx. 40 minutes
508 cal/2136 kJ

Feta

Feta is a cheese made of raw sheep's milk, or occasionally goat's milk. What sets it apart from other cheeses is that it is cubed or cut into squares, then allowed to pickle for about a full month. It therefore tastes lightly sour and salty.

1 Cut the ham into small cubes and mix with the onion-garlic and spice mixes.

2 Clean the mushrooms and cut into small cubes. Crumble the feta and mix with the sesame oil, mushrooms and ham cubes. Season the mix with salt and pepper.

3 Wash and dry the cutlets and cut lengthwise. Spread out over a work surface and cover thinly with the horseradish.

4 Spread the ham mixture over the cutlets and roll them up. Heat the oil in the wok and fry the rolls on all sides.

5 Remove the rolls and clean the wok. Pour the Asia stock into the wok and place the rolls in a bamboo basket.

6 Put the basket in the wok and steam the rolls for 15–20 minutes. Serve the rolls with Hoisin sauce.

LAMB BALLS WITH BEANS

■ Serves 4

3 1/2 oz onion-
garlic mixture
(frozen)

7–8 oz minced
lamb meat

salt

cayenne pepper

3–4 tbsp sesame
seed oil

1 red and 1 yellow
pepper

7 1/2 oz broad
beans (frozen)

2–3 tbsp soy sauce

10 1/2 fl oz
caraway schnapps

7 tbsp lamb stock

Tabasco

Preparation time:
approx. 20 minutes
349 cal/1465 kJ

1 Mix the onion-garlic mixture with the mincemeat. Season the meat well with salt and cayenne pepper, and mould into table-tennis sized balls.

2 Heat the oil in the wok and fry well while stirring. Cut the peppers in two and wash; remove the pips.

3 Cut the peppers into small cubes. Add to the meat in the wok along with the broad beans, fry for a short time.

4 Add the soy sauce, schnapps and lamb stock and braise everything together for 10–15 minutes over a low heat. Season well with Tabasco, dish into bowls and serve.

Broad Beans

These large, kidney-shaped beans are chock full of high-quality protein, carbohydrates and vitamins. When fresh, they must be soaked for 7–8 hours before use. The frozen product is quicker to prepare.

WILD GAME WITH PLUMS

■ Serves 4

14–15 oz
venison filet

4–5 tbsp jarred
plums

7 tbsp wild
game stock

3–4 tbsp plum mash

3–4 tbsp darkbeer

1 tbsp red
wine vinegar

salt

cayenne pepper

ginger, nutmeg and
coriander powder

1/2 bunch
coriander

Preparation time:
approx. 20 minutes
295 cal/1241 kJ

1 Wash and dry the meat and cut into thin slices.

2 Heat the oil in the wok and fry the slices of meat for 3–4 minutes while stirring. Put the plums into a strainer and let drip dry. Add to the meat in the wok and douse with wild game stock.

3 Add the plum mash, darkbeer and vinegar, and braise for 6–8 minutes. Season generously with salt, cayenne pepper, ginger, nutmeg and coriander.

4 Wash and dry the coriander, and chop finely. Dish the meat and serve sprinkled with the coriander.

Darkbeer
This light beer, with its low alcohol content, sets itself apart with its lightly bitter flavour and fruity aftertaste. It goes very well with wild game.

MARINATED MEAT CUBES

■ Serves 4

1 lb 5–6 oz beef filet

3 1/2 oz yoghurt

1/2 tsp cumin

1/2 tsp dried grated lemon grass

1–2 tbsp coriander powder

1 tsp turmeric

salt

1/2 tsp chilli powder

1/2 tsp coarse black pepper

4–5 tbsp peanut oil

2 scallions

1 garlic clove

7 tbsp unsweetened coconut milk

cinnamon and nutmeg powder

Preparation time:
approx. 35 minutes
408 cal/1714 kJ

Turmeric

No spice lends dishes such a spectacular colour as turmeric, also known as curcuma or "yellow spice." The bulbous, concentrated spice, made from a plant in the ginger family, tastes mildly peppery and is easily obtainable anywhere.

1 Wash and dry the beef filet, and cut into small cubes.

2 Stir the yoghurt together with the cumin, lemon grass, coriander powder, turmeric, chilli powder, salt and pepper. Add the meat and let marinate for 10–15 minutes.

3 Heat the oil in the wok and fry the meat cubes with the marinade for 3–5 minutes while stirring.

4 Clean the scallions and cut into rings. Peel the garlic cloves and chop finely. Add both to the meat and fry.

5 Pour in the coconut milk and braise for 3–5 minutes over a low heat. Season with cinnamon and nutmeg, and serve.

STEAMED CABBAGE POCKETS

■ **Serves 4**

8–10 medium-sized savoy cabbages

salt

1 bunch parsley

1 tbsp capers

1 egg

1–2 tbsp grated oregano

1 tsp caraway seeds

onion- and garlic powders

14–15 oz minced pork

cayenne pepper

Preparation time:
approx. 30 minutes
376 cal/1581 kJ

Caraway

The intensive flavour of caraway does more than just lend cabbage dishes that special some-thing; it also helps with digestion. If you do not want to bite your way around the full seeds, you can use ground caraway. This, however, does not possess quite so hearty a flavour as the full seed.

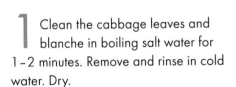

1 Clean the cabbage leaves and blanche in boiling salt water for 1–2 minutes. Remove and rinse in cold water. Dry.

2 Wash and dry the parsley, and chop finely. Chop the capers as well. Knead the meat together with the parsley, capers, eggs, oregano, caraway seeds, and onion- and garlic powder until it becomes a smooth meat batter. Season with salt and pepper and divide onto the cabbage leaves.

3 Pull the edges of the cabbage leaves together and roll them shut. Hold the pockets together with small toothpicks. Bring salt water to the boil in the wok and place the cabbage pockets in the bamboo basket.

4 Put the basket in the wok and steam for 10–15 minutes. Afterwards, re-move the cabbage pockets carefully, dish and serve.

MEDALLIONS WITH OYSTER

■ **Serves 4**

14–15 oz ham filet

4–5 tbsp sesame seed oil

salt

pepper

14–15 oz oyster mushrooms

3 shallots

7 1/4 oz mushroom stock

3 tbsp dry white wine

1 tbsp coarse mustard

1 tsp cornflour

1/2 bunch fresh coriander

Preparation time: approx. 25 minutes
300 cal/1261 kJ

Oyster Mushrooms

The mussel-shaped leaf mushroom wins admirers over with its aromatic, woody flavour. It is quite easy to prepare; because it is usually grown on hay bales, it must simply be rubbed off with a cloth.

1 Wash and dry the meat. Cut into thin medallions.

2 Heat the oil in the wok and fry the medallions on both sides for 2–3 minutes. Season with salt and pepper, remove and keep warm.

3 Clean the mushrooms and cut into small pieces. Peel the shallots and cut into fine cubes. Add the shallots and the mushrooms to the wok and fry for 2–3 minutes.

4 Mix the mushroom stock with the wine, the mustard, the soy sauce and the corn flour. Add to the mushrooms in the wok. Stir while cooking and add the meat once more. Braise for 2–3 minutes.

5 Wash and dry the coriander, and pluck the leaves. Dish the medallions into bowls with the mushrooms, and serve sprinkled with the coriander.

HARE FILET WITH GRAPES

■ Serves 4

10 1/2 oz grapes
1 3/4 oz raisins
14–15 fl oz Armagnac
1/2 tbsp five-spice powder
1 lb 1–2 oz hare filet
2–3 tbsp sesame seed oil
3 1/2 oz bacon bits
salt
pepper
3 1/2 oz lentil sprouts

Preparation time: approx. 30 minutes
347 cal/1459 kJ

1 Wash the grapes, cut them in two and remove the pips. Mix the grapes with the raisins, the Armagnac and the five-spice powder and marinate for 10–15 minutes.

2 Wash and dry the hare filet, and cut into thin strips.

3 Heat the oil in the wok and fry the filet together with the bacon bits for 3–4 minutes while stirring.

4 Add the grape mixture to the wok and braise for another 3–4 minutes. Season generously with the salt and pepper.

5 Wash the lentil sprouts and let drip dry. Add to the wok. Cook for an additional 1–2 minutes while stirring, then dish and serve.

106

Lentil Sprouts
Every health food store and organic grocery offers fresh lentil sprouts. They can, however, also be easily grown at home.

SAVOURY PEPPER STEAK

■ **Serves 4**

1 lb 5–6 oz rump steak

4–5 tbsp sesame seed oil

1 3/4 oz pickled green peppercorns

3 1/2 oz canned mandarins

salt

1/2 bunch chives

Preparation time: approx. 20 minutes
449 cal/1886 kJ

Pepper

The 3- to 4-meter-high pepper plant somewhat resembles the grape vine. White bouquets of flowers appear at the thin, tendrilled ends of the branches twice a year. The green berries, from which green pepper is made, are packed fresh. Black pepper is likewise made of unripe green berries, dried however in the sun and later fermented.

1 Wash and dry the steak, and cut into thin slices. Heat the oil in the wok and fry the slices for 3–4 minutes while stirring.

2 Strain the peppercorns well and add to the wok. Place the mandarins in a strainer and likewise strain. Catch the juice from beneath the strainer.

3 Add the mandarins to the wok and braise for 1–2 minutes. Season with 2–3 tbsp of the mandarin juice and with salt.

4 Wash and dry the chives and cut into fine tubes. Dish up the steak and serve with sprinkled chives.

MEAT-RADISH SALAD

■ **Serves 4**

6 tbsp soy sauce

2–3 tbsp apple vinegar

1 tsp salt

1 tsp sugar

ginger powder

2 dried red chillies, crumbled

2–3 tbsp sesame seeds

2–3 tbsp sesame seed oil

1/2 tsp Wasabi paste

14–15 oz white radish

14–15 oz soured boiled rump

13 fl oz Asia stock

1/2 bunch fresh coriander

Preparation time:
approx. 55 minutes
301 cal/1264 kJ

1 Mix 4 tbsp of the soy sauce with the vinegar, salt, sugar, ginger powder, chilli and sesame seeds. Add the oil slowly while cooking.

2 Add the Wasabi paste and mix in while stirring. Peel the radish and grate coarsely. Place in the marinade and let stand for approximately 30 minutes.

3 Wash and dry the meat, then cut into thin strips. Heat the stock in the wok and cook the meat over a low flame for 15–20 minutes.

4 5 minutes before the meat is done, add the soy sauce. Remove the meat, let drip dry and dip into the radish salad.

5 Wash and dry the coriander, then chop finely. Serve the meat-radish salad lukewarm with coriander as garnish.

Wasabi

The light green Japanese sea radish is available as paste or as powder that can be mixed with water. Be careful when using: Wasabi is fruity, but burning hot.

109

CUTLET WITH MANGELWURZEL

■ **Serves 4**

14–15 oz veal cutlet
salt
pepper
flour
3–4 tbsp peanut oil
1 tbsp chilli oil
1 lb 2 oz mangel-
wurzel
3 shallots
7 tbsp veal stock
3 1/2 oz parma
ham
1 3/4 oz chopped
almonds

Preparation time:
approx. 30 minutes
369 cal/1550 kJ

1 Wash and dry the cutlet, then cut into strips. Dip in salt, pepper and flour.

2 Heat both oils in the wok and fry the meat for 3–4 minutes while stirring. Remove and keep warm.

3 Wash the mangelwurzel and chop finely. Peel the shallots and chop finely. Fry the shallots and mangelwurzel for another 2–3 minutes in the remaining oil.

4 Douse with the veal stock and braise for 4–5 minutes over a low heat. Cut the ham into thin strips and add to the cutlet.

5 Roast the chopped almonds dry in a pan. Serve the cutlet sprinkled with the chopped almonds as garnish.

Mangelwurzel

The tender, dark green leaves of the spinach-like vegetable with the fleshy stem contain large amounts of vitamin A and have a calming effect. The mildly nutty flavour of this vegetable, now nearly forgotten in Europe, makes it worth discovering again.

MINCED BEEF WITH CAPUCINJER

■ **Serves 4**

1 Spanish onion

3 tomatoes

1 green pepper

4–5 tbsp sesame seed oil

1 tsp paprika powder

1 tsp each of cumin, coriander, cardamom and ginger powder

1 tbsp chilli paste

1 lb 2 oz tatar

14–15 oz canned Capucinjer peas

8 tortillas

Preparation time: approx. 30 minutes
509 cal/2138 kJ

1 Peel the onion and cut into small cubes. Cut the tomatoes crosswise, dip in boiling water, rinse in cold water and remove the skin.

2 Remove the pips from the tomatoes and cut the flesh into cubes. Cut the peppers in two, wash them in cold running water and remove the pips. Cut into small cubes.

3 Heat the oil in the wok and fry the onion cubes until glossy. Add the tomato and pepper and fry for another 1–2 minutes. Mix the spices and the chilli paste with the tatar, and mix with the vegetables. Fry for 8–10 minutes while stirring often.

4 Strain the peas, and mix them carefully in with the tatar mix in the wok. Cook for 1–2 minutes. Heat up the tortillas according to the packaging instructions and stuff with the filling. Roll, dish and serve.

Capucinjer Peas
The thick, brown and very mealy peas have
a flavour reminiscent of chickpeas.
Capucinjer peas are found fully cooked
in cans.

LAMB STIR-FRY

■ Serves 4

1 lb 2 oz lamb filet

2–3 tbsp sesame seed oil

salt

pepper

garlic, ginger and cardamom powder

rosemary powder

9 oz mixed pickles

1–2 tbsp sour cream

Preparation time: approx. 40 minutes
267 cal/1121 kJ

Mixed Pickles
The classic assortment of mixed pickles is: silver onions, sweetcorn cauliflower, gherkins, and peppers. Asparagus, beans, mushrooms and carrots are often added to the vinegar as well.

1 Wash and dry the meat, and cut into thin strips. Mix the oil with the spices and marinate the meat in it for 15–20 minutes.

2 Place the meat with the marinade into a heated wok and fry for 5–6 minutes while stirring.

3 Add the mixed pickles with their juice to the wok, and braise for 3–4 minutes. Stir in the sour cream. Dish up the meat and vegetables into bowls and serve.

ASIAN GULASH

■ Serves 4

1 lb 5–6 oz pork

2–3 red onions

2 garlic cloves

3 1/2 oz greens
(frozen)

4–5 tbsp peanut oil

10–15 oz canned
lentils

7 tbsp Asia stock

1–2 tbsp soy sauce

1–2 tbsp apple
vinegar

salt

pepper

nutmeg powder

dash of sugar

1/2 bunch fresh
coriander

Preparation time:
approx. 20 minutes
589 cal/247 kJ

Mien-Sien Noodles

The thin, white shapes
made of wheat flour
and water are usually
offered dried and are
also available as
"Shanghai noodles."

1 Cut the meat into equal-sized cubes.
Peel the onions and garlic and cut into
cubes.

2 Fry the onions and garlic together with
the greens for 2–3 minutes in the
peanut oil. Add the meat and stir while
frying for an additional 3–4 minutes.

3 Strain the lentils, and add to the wok
together with the Asia stock. Braise
for 4–5 minutes over a low heat.

4 Season the gulash with the soy sauce,
the vinegar and the spices until spicy.
Wash and dry the coriander, and chop
finely.

5 Dish up the gulash and serve
garnished with sprinkled coriander.
Mien-Sien noodles are good as a side dish.

COCONUT MEAT BALLS

■ Serves 4

1 bunch scallions

1 fresh ginger root
(1 inch)

14–15 oz mixed
mincemeat

7 1/4 oz minced
lamb

salt

pepper

cumin, garlic and
mustard seed
powder

6–7 tbsp coconut
shavings

4 tbsp peanut oil

17 1/2 fl oz lamb
stock

1 tbsp chilli paste

3–4 tbsp peanut
butter

1 tsp Sambal Oelek

Preparation time:
approx. 30 minutes
575 cal/2418 kJ

Sambal Oelek
One should be careful
when using the spicy
Indonesian pepper
paste on West
European palates. But
in Indonesia it is
sometimes simply
eaten with a spoon.

1 Clean the scallions and cut into small tubes. Peel the ginger and shave finely. Mix both with the mincemeat and the lamb.

2 Season the meat generously with the spices and mould into small-sized balls.

3 Roll the meat balls in the coconut shavings. Heat the oil in the wok and fry the meatballs until golden yellow.

4 Heat up the lamb stock with the chilli paste and the peanut butter while stirring. Flavour with Sambal Oelek and serve the meatballs with the sauce.

DIVERSE: FISH & SEAFOOD

Deep-fried, fried, braised or steamed, in soups, crispy, in filets or curries: no matter how fish- and seafood-lovers like it, the wok is ready to prepare a dazzling array of recipes.

STEAMED CARP

■ Serves 4

2 1/2– 3 1/2 lb
carp (have cut into
pieces at the fish-
monger's)

2–3 tbsp rice wine
or dry sherry

2–3 tbsp coarse sea
salt

2–3 tbsp coarse
pepper

4 shallots

1 fresh ginger root
(2 inches)

2 red peppers

3 1/2 oz canned
bamboo shoots

5–6 tbsp soy sauce

17 1/2 fl oz fish
stock

2–3 tbsp Chinese
mustard

1 tbsp cornflour

2–3 tbsp sour
cream

Preparation time:
approx. 40 minutes
409 cal/1720 kJ

1 Wash the chunks of fish, dry them and douse in rice wine. Rub with salt and pepper and put in a steam basket.

2 Peel the shallots and cut into quarters. Peel the ginger and cut into slices. Clean the peppers, cut them in two and remove the pips. Cut into rectangles.

3 Drain the bamboo shoots in a strainer and mix the vegetables together. Douse with soy sauce.

4 Spread the vegetable mix over the carp. Bring the fish stock to the boil in the wok. Place the steam basket in the wok and steam over a low heat for 15–20 minutes.

5 Remove the basket from the wok and mix the mustard with approximately 12 fl oz fish stock. Mix the cornflour together with a small amount of cold water and use to thicken the fish stock. Taste the sauce and flavour with the sour cream.

6 Arrange the cuts of fish together with the vegetables and the sauce, and serve.

Carp

One of the most beloved of the freshwater fish is the delicious, thick-bodied carp. For fresh, farmed fish, mirror carp are the most widely available today- and not only during Christmas time, but in general from September to April.

LOBSTER CURRY

■ **Serves 4**

2 cooked lobsters (frozen)

4 red onions

3–4 garlic cloves

5–6 tbsp sesame seed oil

ginger and mustard seed powder

cayenne pepper

3 1/2 oz mustard cucumbers

11–12 fl oz unsweetened coconut milk

2 tbsp green curry paste

Preparation time:
approx. 30 minutes
255 cal/1072 kJ

Lobster

The lobster, hummer, or homard is known in any language as the emblem of the gourmet. The meat in the strong pincers and in the tail is especially tasty.

1 Thaw the lobster according to the packaging instructions. Break off the claws and tail and remove the flesh. Cut the lobster meat into small pieces.

2 Peel the onion and garlic and cut both into fine cubes. Heat the sesame oil in the wok and fry the onion and garlic for approximately 2–3 minutes.

3 Season the oil with ginger powder, mustard seed powder and cayenne pepper. Strain the cucumbers well. Cut into fine cubes and add to the wok.

4 Pour in the coconut milk and the curry paste, and stir. Cook for 6–7 minutes over a low heat. Add the lobster meat and cook in the sauce. Ladle into bowls and serve.

CRISPY FISH WITH SESAME

■ Serves 4

17–18 oz saltwater fish

1 tsp salt

1 tsp coarse pepper

2 tbsp sesame seed oil

2–3 tbsp rice wine

1/2 bunch scallions

1 fresh ginger root (1–2 inches)

3 tbsp flour

2–3 eggs

3 1/2 oz white sesame seeds

peanut oil for frying

2 lemons

1/2 bunch parsley

soy sauce

Hoisin sauce

Wasabi

Sambal Oelek

Preparation time: approx. 35 minutes
398 cal/1674 kJ

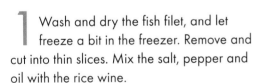

1 Wash and dry the fish filet, and let freeze a bit in the freezer. Remove and cut into thin slices. Mix the salt, pepper and oil with the rice wine.

2 Clean the scallions, and cut into small tubes. Peel the ginger and chop finely. Add the scallions and ginger to the marinade and pour over the filet. Let marinate for 10–15 minutes.

3 Spread the flour over a flat plate. Whisk the eggs and have the sesame seeds handy.

4 Heat enough oil in the wok to fry with. Remove the fish from the marinade and coat each slice in the flour, eggs and sesame seeds. Fry each of the slices in hot oil for 2–3 minutes.

5 Remove the fish crisps from the oil and blot dry with kitchen roll. Cut the lemon into slices. Wash and dry the parsley and pluck the leaves.

6 Serve the crispy fish with lemon slices and parsley as garnish. Soy sauce, Hoisin sauce, Wasabi and Sambal Oelek all make excellent dips.

FINE JACOB'S MUSSELS

■ Serves 4

1 bunch scallions
2 garlic cloves
3 flesh tomatoes
4–5 tbsp sesame oil
salt
pepper
dash of sugar
6–7 oz shelled
Jacob's mussels
3 1/2 oz canned
champignons
7 fl oz sherry
1 tbsp soy sauce

Preparation time:
approx. 20 minutes
468 cal/1966 kJ

1 Clean the scallions and cut into fine rings. Peel the garlic cloves and chop finely.

2 Cut the tomatoes crosswise, dip quickly in boiling water, rinse with cold water and remove the skin. Cut into fine cubes.

3 Heat the oil in the wok and fry the scallions together with the garlic and tomatoes for 2–3 minutes while stirring. Season with salt, pepper and a dash of sugar.

4 Wash and dry the mussels. Cut each in two. Drain the champignons in a strainer. Cut each in two.

5 Add the mussels together with the champignons into the wok and fry for 1 minute, stirring well. Add the sherry and the soy sauce, let simmer and, if desired, season with salt and pepper. Dish up the mussels and serve.

Jacob's Mussels
Jacob's mussels are the symbol and the drinking vessel of the pilgrims to Saint Jacob's grave in Santiago de Compostella. In order to remove fresh mussels from their shells, lay them on a hot plate, so they crack open. Afterwards cut them open lengthwise with a knife and remove the flesh carefully from the shell.

FISH SOUP WITH TOFU

■ Serves 4

1 lb 5–6 oz plaice
filet

1 salad cucumber

3–4 tbsp sesame
seed oil

3 1/2 oz onion-
garlic mix (frozen)

7–8 oz 8-spice-mix
(frozen)

1 pint 15 fl oz
fish stock

1/2 cube crab
soup paste

2–3 tbsp soy sauce

7–8 fl oz aniseed
schnapps

7–8 oz tofu

Preparation time:
approx. 35 minutes
306 cal/1285 kJ

1 Wash and dry the fish filet, and cut into small cubes. Peel the cucumber, cut
in two lengthwise and remove the pips.
Then cut the cucumber into triangles.

2 Heat the oil in the wok and fry the fish
cubes together with the cucumber triangles for 2–3 minutes. Add the onion-garlic mix and the 8-spice mix.

3 Pour in the stock and crumble the crab
paste with the soup. Let dissolve while
stirring.

4 Season the soup with the soy sauce
and the aniseed schnapps. Cook for
10 minutes over a low heat.

5 Slice the tofu into small pieces and
add to the wok 3 minutes before finish-
ing cooking. Ladle the soup into bowls and
serve.

Plaice

Plaice is the most popular flatfish
in these parts.
The tender, white filets of this flat,
salt-water fish are rich in taste and
low in calories.

127

DEEP-FRIED SARDINES

■ Serves 4

1 lb 12–13 oz
ready-prepared
sardines
ginger and chilli
powder
1/2 tsp turmeric
flour for breading
1 bunch coriander
3 egg yolks
3–4 oz flour
5–9 fl oz pils beer
peanut oil for frying
1 fresh lemon
a few leaves of lollo
bianco for garnish

Preparation time:
approx. 30 minutes
458 cal/1925 kJ

Sardines
Sardines are small her-
ring fish with fatty, spicy
and slightly salty flesh.
They are most
well-known tinned in
oil, but it is well worth
it to give fresh ones
a try as well.

1 Wash and dry the sardines, and rub
with ginger- and chilli powder and
turmeric. Dip in flour and have ready to
use.

2 Wash the coriander, dry well and roll
the individual stalks in the flour as
well. Whisk the egg yolks, and mix in the
flour and the beer.

3 Heat the oil in the wok. Dust off the ex-
cess flour from the sardines and the
coriander, and dip them in the batter.

4 Fry the fish and the coriander in hot
peanut oil portion by portion.

5 Rub off the lemon with a towel and
cut fine strips from the rind with a
lemon peeler. Arrange the sardines with the
coriander sprigs. Garnish with the lemon
rind and the lollo bianco, and serve.

FRIED SEAFOOD

■ Serves 4

1 lb 12–13 oz seafood (frozen)

1–2 tbsp five-spice powder

1 sprig rosemary

1/2 bunch thyme

1 tbsp lemon juice

1 tbsp capers

1 oz black pitted olives

7–8 oz dried tomatoes packed in oil

4–5 tbsp peanut oil

7–14 oz grappa

Preparation time: approx. 25 minutes
409 cal/1720 kJ

Seafood

The mixture of flavourful seafood is pre-prepared and deep frozen before being sold in markets, and is ideal for all types of preparation styles. In the wok especially, Seafood is quickly prepared in a variety of ways.

1 Thaw the seafood according to preparation instructions. Sprinkle with the five-spice powder and let stand for approximately 5 minutes.

2 Wash and dry the herbs, pluck the leaves and chop finely. Stir the herbs together with the lemon juice and the well-drained capers. Cut the olives into small pieces and add to the lemon juice mix.

3 Drain the tomatoes well in a strainer. Chop into large chunks and likewise add to the herb mixture.

4 Heat the oil in the wok and fry the seafood for 3–4 minutes while stirring. Remove and keep warm.

5 Fry the herb-olive-tomato mix in the leftover oil for 3–4 minutes. Return the seafood to the wok and cook for 1 minute. Flavour with the grappa, arrange and serve. If desired, sprinkle with chives as a garnish.

BRAISED EEL WITH FENNEL

■ **Serves 4**

1 lb 12 oz eel

4–5 tbsp sherry vinegar

1 tbsp coarse sea salt

1 3/4 oz pickled ginger

7–8 oz parsnip

10–11 oz fennel

6–7 tbsp sesame seed oil

1 tbsp fennel seeds

salt

cayenne pepper

5–9 fl oz fish stock

1/2 bunch parsley

lemon rinds for garnish

Preparation time: approx. 35 minutes

293 cal/1232 kJ

Parsnip
The yellowish roots, reminiscent of carrots, have an aromatic, sweet and spicy flavour. Parsnips can be cooked as a carrot-like vegetable, but are ideal raw in a salad as well.

1 Wash the eel and cut into 2- or 3-inch-wide pieces. Douse with the vinegar and sprinkle with the sea salt. Let stand for 5–8 minutes.

2 Place the ginger in a strainer and drain well. Wash the fennel and parsnip, and cut into bits.

3 Heat the oil in the wok and fry the eel pieces for 4–5 minutes while stirring. Add the ginger, parsnip, fennel and fennel seeds and fry for and additional 3–4 minutes. Season with salt and cayenne pepper, and pour in the fish stock. Braise over low heat for 6–8 minutes.

4 Wash and dry the parsley, and pluck the leaves from the stems. Arrange the braised eel with the parsley and lemon rinds, and serve.

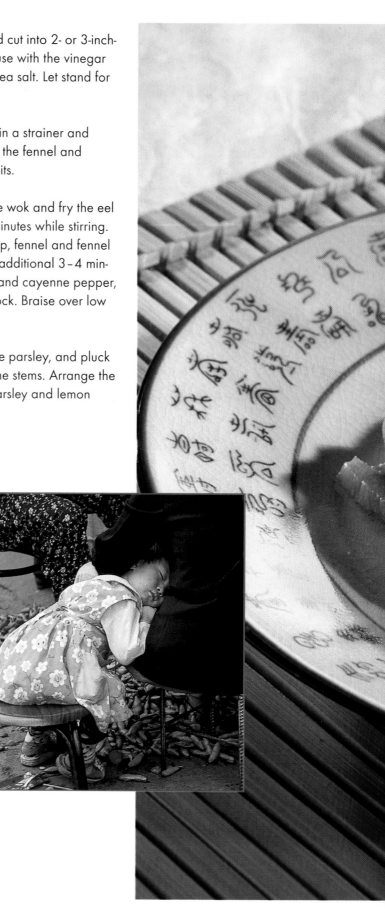

CRAYFISH WITH ARTICHOKE

■ **Serves 4**

2–3 lb crayfish (frozen, cooked in the shell)

2 garlic cloves

4 shallots

coriander, cumin and ginger powder

1 tbsp chilli sauce

4–5 tbsp sesame seed oil

10–14 oz canned artichoke hearts

7 tbsp Asia stock cornflour

Preparation time:
approx. 30 minutes
427 cal/1793 kJ

1 Thaw the crayfish according to packaging instructions. Break the tails off and apart, and remove the flesh. Cut the meat into pieces.

2 Peel the garlic cloves and the shallots and cut into small cubes. Mix both with the crayfish meat and season with the spices and the chilli sauce.

3 Heat the oil in the wok and fry the crayfish and mixture for 3–4 minutes while stirring.

4 Drain the artichoke hearts in a strainer and let drip dry. Cut the hearts into small cubes and add together with the Asia stock into the wok. Braise for 1–2 minutes over mild heat.

5 Mix the corn flour with a small amount of cold water and use this to thicken the crayfish-artichoke mixture. Arrange the crayfish with the artichokes, and serve.

Crayfish

Crayfish live in fresh water and 30 to 50 years ago they still cavorted in every clean, native stream and river. Now they are mostly imported from China and from South- and Southeast Europe, usually cooked from frozen.

FRIED FISH CUTS

■ **Serves 4**

1 lb 2 oz fish filet
(frozen)

3 1/2 oz garlic-
onion mix (frozen)

3 1/2 oz herb de
provence (frozen)

3 1/2 oz bacon bits

salt

pepper

ginger and mustard-
seed powder

2–3 eggs

1 medium-sized
baguette

1 1/2 oz–3 1/2 oz
sesame seeds

peanut oil for frying

1 lemon

plum sauce

Preparation time:
approx. 35 minutes
514 cal/2160 kJ

1 Thaw the fish filet, and feed through the fine-grained side of the mincer along with the garlic-onion mix and the herbs de provence. Knead the bacon into the minced filet.

2 Season the minced filet with salt, pepper, ginger and mustard-seed powder. Whisk the eggs. Cut the bread into thin slices and cut slices into the crust on all sides.

3 Batter the slices of bread with the egg. Divide the fish mash onto the slices and sprinkle with sesame seed.

4 Press the fish well into the bread and again batter with egg. Heat the oil in the wok. Lay the bread slices with the fish mash downwards onto a straining spoon, and dip in the oil. Fry over a low heat for 3–4 minutes, until crispy.

5 Blot the fish cuts on kitchen roll. Cut the lemon into eighths. Garnish the fish cuts with the lemon and serve. Serve the plum sauce separately. Fried Asian mushrooms go well as a side dish.

FINE GARLIC PRAWNS

■ Serves 4

2 lb–2 lb 4 oz
giant prawn tails,
raw in the shell

sesame oil for deep
frying

10 garlic cloves

3–4 red chilli
peppers

1 bunch scallions

lemon pepper

3 1/2 oz sweet and
sour packed ginger

2 tbsp peanut oil

Preparation time:
approx. 35 minutes
499 cal/2097 kJ

1 Wash and dry the giant prawn, and deep fry in hot sesame oil for 40–50 seconds, until they are fully red. Remove and blot on kitchen roll.

2 Peel and crush the garlic. Cut the chillies in two, rinse under cold running water and remove the pips. Cut into small rings.

3 Rinse the scallions, cut them into rings and mix with the garlic cloves and the chilli rings. Season with lemon pepper.

4 Mince the ginger and add to the scallion-garlic mixture. Heat the peanut oil in the wok and fry the mixture while stirring for 3–4 minutes.

5 Add the prawn and stir into the mix for 1–2 minutes. Dish up and serve with lime.

Giant Prawn

Whether giant prawn, king prawn, gamba or crevette-these shrimps can grow to weigh up to 9 ounces.

SALMON WEST INDIAN STYLE

■ **Serves 4**

**4 salmon filets
(each 5–6 oz)**

**4–5 tbsp lemon
juice**

**14–15 fl oz
white rum**

**2–3 tbsp lemon
pepper**

1 bunch scallions

4–5 garlic cloves

1 mango

2 oz butter oil

**5–6 oz fresh shelled
shrimp**

**8–9 fl oz unsweet-
ened coconut milk**

1–2 tbsp hot salsa

Preparation time:
approx. 35 minutes
607 cal/2550 kJ

Salmon

The lighter in the colour
the flesh of the salmon,
the fattier and tastier it is.
Salmon should always
be prepared fresh if
possible and should
not be kept longer
than one day in the
refrigerator.

1 Wash and dry the salmon. Baste with the lemon juice and the rum. Season the filets with the lemon pepper. Let infuse for 20–25 minutes.

2 Clean the scallions and cut into rings. Peel the garlic cloves and chop into fine bits. Peel the mango, free the flesh from the pit and cut into cubes.

3 Heat the butter oil in the wok and braise the salmon together with the shrimp. Add the scallions, garlic and mango. Fry for another 4 minutes or so.

4 Douse the contents of the wok with the coconut milk and add the salsa. Stew for 2–3 minutes over a low heat. Dish everything up together and serve. Wild rice goes well as a side dish.

SEA BASS ROLLS

■ Serves 4

1 courgette

3 tomatoes

2 thin leeks

3 carrots

7 1/4 oz giant
mushrooms

3 1/2 oz cooked
ham

1 tbsp five-spice
powder

3–4 tbsp sesame
seed oil

4 sea bass filets
(each 7–8 oz)

1–2 tbsp Wasabi

1–1 1/2 pint fish
stock

2–3 tbsp soy sauce

Preparation time:
approx. 35 minutes
239 cal/1379 kJ

1 Wash the courgette, and cut into small cubes. Peel and pit the tomatoes, and cut also into cubes.

2 Wash the leeks, and chop these finely as well. Peel and cube the carrots. Clean the mushrooms and chop into small pieces.

3 Slice the ham into thin strips. Flavour the vegetables with the five-spice powder. Heat the oil in the wok and fry the vegetables together with the gammon for 4–5 minutes while stirring.

4 Wash the fish filets and cut diagonally into thin slices. Brush the slices of flesh with a thin layer of Wasabi and set into the wok with the vegetables and ham.

5 Roll up the fish slices and set fast with toothpicks. Heat the fish stock with the soy sauce in the wok.

6 Place the fish rolls into a bamboo basket and set the basket into the wok. Steam for 4–5 minutes over a low heat. Remove the basket, arrange the fish rolls and serve. Basmati rice is a suitable side dish.

Sea Bass

The "wolf of the sea" is a delectable fish, but not a very cheap one. In recipes, it can be replaced by herring filets, gilthead or other salt-water fish.

SWEET AND SOUR LEMON FISH

■ Serves 4

1 lb 1–2 oz shallots

5–6 tbsp peanut oil

6 tbsp sherry vinegar

9 fl oz fish stock

1 crushed bay leaf

nutmeg, mustard seed and ginger powder

coarse black pepper

1–2 dried pressed chillies

1 tsp thyme shavings

salt

sugar

1 lb 1–2 oz fish filet

2 tsp cornflour

Preparation time:
approx. 25 minutes
342 cal/1438 kJ

Sherry Vinegar
This aromatic vinegar is especially well suited to fried fish dishes, poultry, vegetables and salads. Be sparing with the vinegar, and use diluted.

1 Peel the shallots and cut into cubes. Heat the peanut oil in the wok and fry the shallots for 5–6 minutes.

2 Add the vinegar, fish stock, bay leaf, spice powders, chillies, thyme, salt and sugar to the wok and cook for another 6–8 minutes over a low heat.

3 Wash and dry the fish filet and cut into small cubes. Coat with the cornflour.

4 Add the fish to the wok. Cook for 5–6 minutes while stirring. Arrange the onion and fish with the sauce and serve. As a side dish, use rice.

COLOURFUL CALAMARI

■ **Serves 4**

1 lb 1–2 oz Chinese mixed vegetables

3 1/2 oz canned water chestnuts

3 1/2 oz canned bamboo shoots

3 1/2 oz canned palm hearts

6–7 tbsp sesame seed oil

ginger, garlic and onion powder

salt

pepper

1lb small squid

1/2 bunch coriander

Preparation time: approx. 30 minutes
304 cal/1276 kJ

Calamari

You can purchase these tiny squid in Europe ready to prepare or as a frozen product. Because they require a very short cooking time, calamari lend themselves well to stir-frying.

1 Allow the Chinese vegetables to thaw a bit. Drain the water chestnuts, bamboo shoots and palm hearts in a strainer. Cut them into fine slices.

2 Heat the oil in the wok and fry all the vegetables for 4–5 minutes while stirring. Season with the spices, salt and pepper.

3 Add the calamari to the wok and fry for an additional 3–4 minutes while stirring. Wash and dry the coriander, and pluck the leaves.

4 Arrange the calamari on plates and serve sprinkled with coriander.

STEAMED PERCH

■ **Serves 4**

8–9 oz lotus roots

8–9 oz salad cucumbers

8–9 oz carrots

5 tbsp apple vinegar

8–9 fl oz vegetable stock

2–3 tsp sugar

1/2 tsp salt

8 bamboo leaves

1 lb 1–2 oz sea perch filet

2–3 tbsp sesame seed oil

2–3 tbsp ginger juice

2–3 tbsp Mirin

8–9 oz jarred mussels

Preparation time:
approx. 40 minutes
406 cal/1706 kJ

Sea Perch

The fine, firm and aromatic flesh of the sea perch is rich in nutrients, low in calories and also easily digestible. The best way to prepare the perch is to steam it sparingly in the steam basket.

1 Peel the lotus roots and carve ring shapes into them between the hollows. Then cut into thin rings.

2 Peel the cucumber and the carrot and cut into thin slices. Mix the apple vinegar with the vegetable stock and the spices.

3 Bring the mixture to the boil in the wok. Add the prepared vegetables and cook for 5–6 minutes over a low heat. Then remove the vegetables and let drip dry.

4 Wash and dry the perch filet. Stir the oil together with the ginger juice and the Mirin, and marinate the filets for 4–5 minutes in it. Drain the mussels.

5 Divide the vegetables onto the bamboo leaves. Lay the filets on top with the marinade and lay the mussels over this. Fold the bamboo leaves over and place the packets in the steam basket.

6 Bring the vegetable stock once more to the boil and put the basket in the wok. Steam while covered for around 10 minutes. Dish up the perch and serve.

REFINED FISH BALLS

■ Serves 4

1 bunch scallions
3–4 garlic cloves
3–4 chillies
1 lb 12–13 oz sea
fish filet
salt, pepper
1 tbsp dried grated
lemon grass
1 tbsp ginger
powder
1 tsp turmeric
4–5 tbsp peanut oil
12–13 fl oz
unsweetened
coconut milk
1 tbsp creamed
coconut
1 tbsp chilli sauce
sweet and sour
sauce

Preparation time:
approx. 30 minutes
855 cal/3592 kJ

1 Wash and dry the scallions and cut into bits. Peel the garlic. Cut the chillies in two, wash under cold running water and remove the seeds.

2 Wash and dry the fish filet, and cut into pieces. Feed the fish together with the scallions, garlic cloves and chillies through the fine side of the mincer.

3 Season the fish mash with the spices and mould into small balls. Heat the oil in the wok and fry the fish balls portion by portion for 5–6 minutes. Remove and keep warm.

4 Stir the coconut milk together with the creamed coconut and the chilli sauce into the remaining cooking oil. Add the fish balls again and cook over a low heat for around 10 minutes. Dish up the fish balls with the sauce and, if desired, serve with the sweet and sour sauce.

Tip
The fish balls gain an exceptionally
succulent flavour when prepared from half
fish and half prawn, or one third fish, one
third prawn and one third smoked Chinese
gammon from an Asian import store.

HALIBUT WITH SPROUTS

■ Serves 4

1 lb 12–13 oz
halibut
lemon juice
salt
pepper
5–6 sesame seed oil
7–8 oz canned
kidney beans
1 lb 1–2 oz power-
sprout mix
2–3 tbsp soy sauce
2–3 Nori leaves

Preparation time:
approx. 25 minutes
482 cal/2024 kJ

Sprout Mix
Fresh sprouts are
available in health food
stores and organic
groceries. The power
sprout mix contains
sprouts of wheat,
adzuki beans, mung
beans, alfalfa, radish
and onion.

1 Wash and dry the halibut. Cut into
slices. Douse the fish with lemon juice
and season with salt and pepper.

2 Heat the oil in the wok and fry the
fish portion by portion for about
4 minutes. Drain the kidney beans in a
strainer. Rinse the sprouts with cold water
and likewise drain.

3 Add the beans and the sprouts to the
fish in the wok and fry for another
3–4 minutes while stirring. Season with the
soy sauce.

4 Roast the Nori leaves dry in a pan
on one side, then crumble. Dish the
halibut, sprinkle with the Nori flakes, garnish with lemon slices and parsley if desired, and serve.

GOURMET SCRAMBLED EGG

■ Serves 4

4–5 tbsp sesame
seed oil

7 1/4 oz coarsely-
chopped spinach
(frozen)

1 3/4 oz onion-gar-
lic mix (frozen)

7 1/4 oz Shiitake
mushrooms

4–5 tbsp rice wine

7 1/4 oz shelled,
cooked giant prawn

5–6 eggs

mineral water

salt, pepper

cardamom powder

Keta caviar for
garnish

Preparation time:
approx. 25 minutes
427 cal/1793 kJ

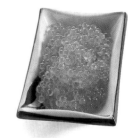

Caviar

Caviar is the collective
term for the flavourful
eggs of fish and other
seafood. Unlike the
black or grey caviar
from many other kinds of
fish, that of the Keta fish
shimmers red.

1 Heat the oil in the wok and fry the spinach together with the onion-garlic mix for 5–6 minutes. Clean the mushrooms, cut into slices and add to the wok. Fry for another 2–3 minutes while stirring.

2 Add the rice wine and the prawns, and braise for 2–3 minutes over low heat. Whisk the eggs with a bit of mineral water. Season with salt, pepper and cardamom, and add to the prawns and vegetables in the wok.

3 Simmer for around 7 minutes and stir continually. Dish the scrambled egg onto plates and serve garnished with caviar.

SWEET & FRUITY

The wok is also up for the challenge of preparing succulent desserts. Whether made with bananas, apples, coconut or pumpkin, the result is always a sweet, alluring temptation.

STEAMED FRUIT WAN TANS

■ Serves 4

4 oz flour
1 1/2 tsp sugar
1/2 tsp lard
1 apple
1 pear
1 tbsp lemon juice
4 canned peach halves
1 baby pineapple
2–3 tbsp honey
1–2 tbsp cinnamon sugar
2–3 tbsp crushed almonds
1 tbsp additional sugar

Preparation time:
approx. 35 minutes
330 cal/1389 kJ

Cinnamon Sugar
It is always best to prepare one's own cinnamon sugar: mix 1 tsp cinnamon powder to each 1/3 cup cane sugar. In well-sealed containers, cinnamon sugar keeps its aroma for 1–2 months.

1 Sift the flour into a bowl. Add 1/2 tbsp sugar. Warm 3 tbsp water and stir in with the flour.

2 Knead into one solid dough. Roll the dough razor-thin on a floured work surface. Slice the dough into 12 equally-sized rectangles.

3 Peel the apple and the pear, remove the pips from both and grate finely. Douse immediately with the lemon juice. Drain the peach halves, and cut into small cubes. Peel the pineapple, remove the stalk and cut likewise into small cubes.

4 Mix the honey together with the cinnamon sugar and the crushed almonds. Add the fruit and spoon the mixture into the middle of each rectangle of dough. Pull the four corners together.

5 Put the wan tans in a steam basket. Bring water to the boil with the rest of the sugar in the wok. Put the basket in the wok and steam while covered for 10–12 minutes over a low heat. Dish the wan tans onto plates and serve.

BAKED CINNAMON APPLES

■ Serves 4

2–3 apples

2–3 tbsp lemon juice

1–2 tbsp cinnamon sugar

6 tbsp whole wheat flour

2 eggs

1 pinch salt

1–2 tbsp sesame seeds

peanut oil for frying

5–6 oz sour cream
or
5–6 tbsp maple syrup

Preparation time:
approx. 35 minutes
437 cal/1835 kJ

1 Peel the apple, cut out the core and slice the apple into 1-inch-thick rings. Douse immediately with the lemon juice. Then sprinkle with the cinnamon sugar and let stand for 5–6 minutes to absorb flavour.

2 For the dough, mix the flour together with the eggs, the salt and the sesame seeds. Heat a sufficient amount of oil in the wok. Dip the apple slices in the dough and fry portion by portion in the hot oil.

3 Dish the apple slices either with sour cream or maple syrup, and serve.

Maple Syrup

The syrup from the sap of the maple tree is especially beloved in North America as a sweetener. The dark, gold-brown syrup has a lightly sour secondary flavour and a lower sugar content than honey. After opening, it must be kept refrigerated.

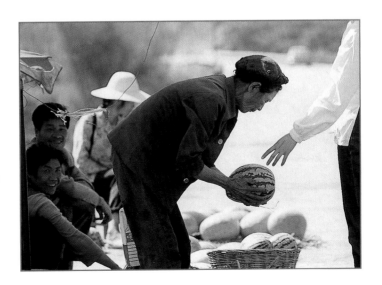

BANANA CRISPS

■ Serves 4

3 1/2 oz brown
cane sugar

1–2 tsp each of
orange and lemon
peel flavouring

1 3/4 oz ground
unsalted peanuts

10 bananas

2–3 tbsp lemon
juice

3 1/2 oz coconut oil
for frying

Preparation time:
approx. 35 minutes
624 cal/2620 kJ

Bananas

Bananas contain
vitamins and minerals,
especially vitamin B 6,
which is good for the
blood and for protein
exchange.

1 Mix the sugar together with the orange- and lemon extract and the peanuts. Peel the bananas and cut into slices. Douse immediately with lemon juice.

2 Heat the coconut oil in the wok. Dip the banana slices in the sugar mix and fry portion by portion in the hot coconut oil.

3 Remove the banana crisps from the oil and let cool on a cooling rack. Watch that the bananas do not stick together.

PUMPKIN-CARROT POCKETS

■ **Serves 4**

12 rice leaves

7–8 oz sweet and
sour preserved
pumpkin

3 1/2 oz sweet and
sour preserved
ginger

7–8 oz carrots

6 tbsp brown sugar

2–3 tbsp milk

cardamom, ginger
and aniseed
powder

1 3/4 oz raisins

1 pinch saffron

1 3/4 oz grated
pecan nuts

1 3/4 oz butter

3–4 tbsp ginger jam

1 tbsp sugar

1/2 bunch lemon
balm

Preparation time:
approx. 40 minutes
365 cal/1536 kJ

1 Lay the rice leaves on a damp towel and allow them to absorb moisture, so that they are malleable. Drain the pumpkin and the ginger in a strainer.

2 Cut the pumpkin and the ginger into small cubes. Peel and grate the carrots. Mix the grated carrot into the ginger and pumpkin mix.

3 Add the sugar, milk and spices, and stir. Add the raisins, saffron and pecan nuts as well.

4 Spread the rice leaves on a work surface and divide the pumpkin-ginger mix onto them. Stir the butter with the ginger jam and spread on the pockets.

5 Pull the leaves into bags and set in the steam basket. Bring sugar water to the boil in the wok. Set the steam basket in the wok and steam for 10–15 minutes while covered.

6 Wash and dry the lemon balm and pluck the leaves. Garnish the pockets with the balm and serve.

Cardamom
Of the green and black
varieties, the wizened
pollen of the green,
three-sided capsules
is preferred in Asia for
curries, vegetable
dishes and pastries.

COCONUT-FRUIT OMELETTES

■ **Serves 4**

4 Sharon fruits
2 kiwis
2 guavas
2–3 tbsp brown sugar
3 1/2 oz creamed coconut
3 1/2 oz coconut shavings
4–6 eggs
mineral water
2–3 tbsp coconut oil for frying

Preparation time:
approx. 30 minutes
404 cal/1696 kJ

1 Remove the Sharon fruits from their stems and peel. Cut the fruit into cubes.

2 Peel the kiwis and the guavas, and cut into cubes. Mix the fruit with the sugar, creamed coconut and coconut shavings.

3 Beat the eggs for 2–3 minutes until frothy, and add a bit of mineral water.

4 Heat the oil in the wok and make thin omelettes from the batter. Let the omelettes dry on paper towels, divide the fruit among them, fold together dish up and serve.

Sharon Fruit

The orange-coloured, tomato-sized fruits - named after the stretch of coast between Tel Aviv and the Carmel Mountains-are eaten like apples. They can be eating raw as well as in desserts or as additions to poultry dishes.

BATATA BALLS

■ **Serves 4**

1 lb 2 oz canned batatas

3–4 tbsp poppy seeds

1 tbsp whole wheat flour

1–2 tbsp cane sugar

1–2 eggs

ginger, cardamom and nutmeg powder

vanilla extract

3 1/2 oz coconut oil for frying

icing sugar

Preparation time:
approx. 35 minutes
522 cal/2192 kJ

1 Drain the batatas in a strainer. Mash with a fork.

2 Mix the poppy seeds together with the flour and the sugar in with the batata mash. Whisk the eggs and add them to the mix as well. Season the mash with the spice powders and mould into small balls.

3 Heat the oil in the wok and fry the balls until golden yellow. Drip dry on kitchen roll and serve sprinkled with icing sugar.

Batatas

This tropical tuber, a type of sweet potato, is known for its high starch- and sugar content, as well as vitamins A and C. The flour made from batata is superb for thickening soups, sauces and other sweet dishes.